Zen of Cubing

In Search of the Seventh Side

Happy Jack Feder & Kathryn West Merrick

Zen of Cubing

In Search of the Seventh Side

Happy Jack Feder & Kathryn West Merrick

Illustrations by Christopher Merrick

South Bend, Indiana

ZEN OF CUBING

and books
702 South Michigan, South Bend, Indiana 46618

Library of Congress Catalog Number: 82-072610

International Standard Book Number: 0-89708-103-X

First Edition

Printed in the United States of America

Additional copies available:
    the distributors
    702 South Michigan
    South Bend, Indiana 46618

To Our Parents,

Jack and Patty

&

Art and June

The cube is the only thing you didn't teach us to solve!

Contents

Introduction

Why be embarrassed? There are at least ten million others like you. You've purchased a cube and you haven't 'solved' it. Really, there's no need to be embarrassed. We haven't solved it either. But that's no reason to hate the little thing. You don't need to smash it with a hammer, commit mental suicide or give it to your mother-in-law with the weak heart. You can still have fun with it. Join the Zen of Cubing club!

The Zen of Cubing can be practiced by everyone; both by the small elite group of Cubbhist Masters who *actually* have solved the Cube, as well as the great majority of us who are totally unsuccessful and inept at solving it. Everyone can derive pleasure from the Cube, even if only as a rationalization for repeated failures. In this way, Cubbhists today number well over twenty million!

This book will help all Cubies to gain fuller enjoyment of all aspects of the Cube, all except the technical aspects of solving it. We've written *The Zen of Cubing* as a guide for all to learn about the Holistic approach to Cubing; including directions towards relating with the Cube through intimate, sensual joys. Browse through the *L.L. Cube Catalog* section for fun and exciting cube accessories, and discover the official likes and dislikes of many Zen Cubies. If you now own a Cube, remember that by simply investing your money in a Cube and having failed to solve it does not mean that you should not derive pleasure from it! Our guiding motto is: Why growl with frustration when you can laugh with mindless pleasure?

1
Timely Tales of the Cube

THE CREATION THEORY

In the beginning, all was Chaos. Matter flew wildly about, light did not shine, and shrill dissonant sounds pierced space.

The Supreme One gazed with disgust at this disorder. "This shall not be!" he commanded, and it was thus. From the matter he formed planets, stars, comets and deep space radio waves. From the shrill dissonant sounds he made the cheery chirps of birds and the rustle of trees blowing in the warm wind. From the darkness he made light, and with that light, rainbows and the aurora borealis.

Chaos ceased to exist.

But the Supreme One grew lonely, so he made Adam, a good friend. When Adam grew lonely, He made Eve, a good mate. Adam and Eve cherished each other and their paradise. They had to but follow one rule: *Never touch the holy Cube of Six Colors.*

"It is the symbol of my Supreme Power," He said. "It represents my control over chaos, a power I have exerted because of my love for you."

That sounded good to both Adam and Eve.

One day the two were sitting around, not really bored, but with a lot of time to kill, nonetheless. They looked at the many colored, many faceted Cube. "I don't see what the big deal is," said Eve.

"Better not to think about it," murmured Adam.

"But wouldn't it look a lot more interesting if this red square was in the middle of the blues and the blue square in the middle of the reds?"

"Well, maybe..."

Several hours later, Eve said to Adam, "Oops." Adam made a shrill dissonant sound. The Supreme One heard this sound of Chaos and knew at once what had happened. He grew angry.

"I have given you Utopia and you have forsaken it. I have given you order and you have recreated Chaos. For this I shall banish you from my paradise."

The next day, Adam was still trying to restore the Cube to it's original state. His stomach growled. He looked up at Eve and saw that she was wearing fig leaves.

"Say, what are you hiding behind those leaves?"

When she showed him, he quickly tossed the Cube of Six Colors away and never again looked at it.

He did not have much use for the Cube.

THE EVOLUTION THEORY

Monkeys swung from the trees in the jungles of primeval eastern Africa. They chittered and chattered and picked lice off one another. Some of them slept in secure little nooks in the upper branches of trees. Others played with cubes.

They'd spin the sides about to make fun new shapes and combinations of colors. They didn't try to get the same color on

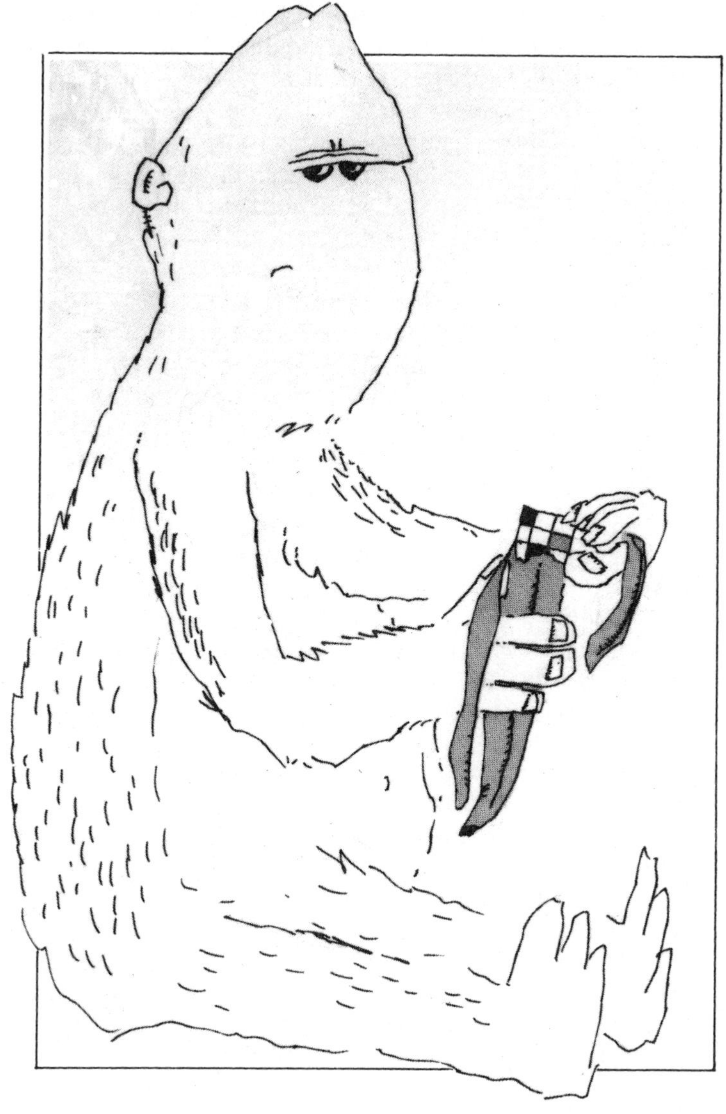

all nine squares of each of the six sides — the concept that it could be done was beyond their grasp. When they tired of changing colors they would do other fun things like try to stick the cube in their ears, chew on it, or smash it with a green banana. When enemies approached their territory, they would pelt them with cubes and drive them away.

One historic day (appoximately 300,000 BC, according to the 1954 arcubology dig at O'Cubeye Gorge, under the direction of Boxford University) one monkey looked at his friends and mates, and saw them all whiling away the day and playing with cubes. That didn't set right with him. "Rrrrreeechuchusss!" he screamed. Roughly translated, this means "Why do you waste your life on silly things like this cube when you could be building shoe factories, forming governments, dumping toxic wastes into the rivers, and struggling to pay taxes?" His monkey friends hardly noticed. They chittered about and continued playing with their cubes. Except for one young female.

She walked up to him (on her hind legs) and said, "Rrrreeeechuchus." This is exactly what he had said, but she used a different intonation. The one she used meant, "You're right. I'd be willing to give up my equality with the others in this tribe and join you. Together we can create a society where I can be your servant and slave. I can mend your clothes, drive the kids to school, drive you to work, stand in line for expensive groceries, stand in line at the bank, clean the house, fight the traffic and pick you up from work, get the kids from school, cook your dinner, wash the clothes, get the kids to bed, and then try to find some time to pick you clean of lice."

That sounded great to him. He told her she would have to leave her cube behind. She obeyed. They were to be the first humans, and unlike monkeys, would not have much use for the cube.

EGYPT AND THE GREAT CUBOIDS

The young boy Pharoah watched with growing despair as each of his fifty most intelligent slaves struggled vainly to solve as many cubes. His despair soon turned to anger and he stomped his staff on the floor of solid gold. "Bring me the court architect!" he screamed.

Moments later the breathless architect arrived. Though a proud man, he fell prostrate before his lord, the boy Pharoah. "What is your wish, most worshipped one?"

The Pharoah bade him to rise. "I wish a tomb built for my journey across the river Styx."

"As you command," answered the architect. "I shall build a glorious tomb. A huge Pyramid!" His mind raced with the joy of the challenging prospect — and with the pride of knowing he was the *only* architect who could properly design such a magnificent structure.

"No," said the boy Pharoah, "I desire a Great Cuboid. A huge cube of limestone, each side painted a solid color. This will ensure me of the skill I need to solve the cube on the other side."

The architect was incredulous. His professional pride had been insulted. A cube? For a tomb? As much as he loved the boy Pharoah, he could not help but laugh. "Are you crazed? A square block? What beauty is in that? What preservative powers does it hold?"

The boy Pharoah made a secret gesture to a well muscled man holding a giant sword. The architect continued to scoff. "Why, any child could design a Cube. I have no use for cubes!" But before the architect could utter another word, the Pharoah's servant sliced off his head with a great swing.

The architect may have been wrong in laughing at the boy Pharoah, but he had been right about one thing.

With his head rolling on the golden floor, he indeed did not have much use for cubes....

CUSTER'S LAST CUBE

General George Armstrong Custer and his division of U.S. Cavalry were fighting off a vicious assault by a group of recalcitrant Indians. Or rather, Custer's men were fighting it out. the General sat on a weathered log and pondered his next move on the cube.

"Sir, excuse me." Custer looked up at the man who addressed him. It was that rude sergeant, panting and bleeding. Custer snapped at him. "You call yourself a sergeant? Look at you! You're a mess. Can't even dodge an arrow."

"But sir, we're outnumbered ten to one, and we have poor field positions. If we don't retreat we'll..."

"Poppycock!" Custer looked back down at his cube. "Oh, finnagle. You've made me forget my next move. This is going on your record, sergeant."

"Yes, sir."

Custer held his cube up and began pontificating. "This little contraption is the difference between the white man and the red man. The red man hasn't the reasoning faculties to comprehend such marvels. The white man, however, finds himself in need of such in order to..."

At that moment an arrow went through the heart of George Custer. It was a bad day all around. His first mistake was in his battle strategy. His second mistake was to think that he needed the cube. After the Battle, one Indian brave lifted his scalp and caught sight of the General's cube. With a chuckle he tossed the scalp on the ground and picked up the cube. He found it much more interesting than the General's dirty scalp. He walked away playing with the cube.

"After all," said the Indian, "The General will not have much use for a cube."

Not long after the brave showed the cube to other tribes, the Indians allowed themselves to be peacefully relocated to reservations.

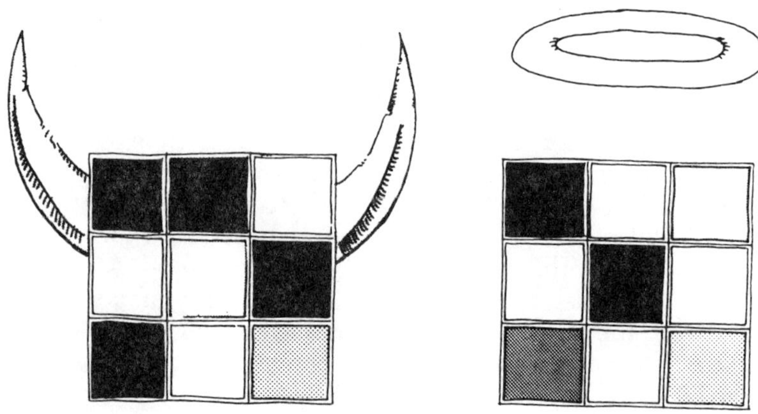

CONTEMPORARY LIFE

Modern people have little need of the cube. Today, we have fast and luxurious cars, stereo systems, slow mail service and prepackaged foods. We have geothermal power, nuclear power, hydroelectric power, and for a short time we even had flower power.

Like Adam and Eve, we have little use for a cube. Certainly less use for a cube than the boy Pharaoh's architect. The monkeys, by all reasoning, should have been able to make more use of a cube than modern man. Whether or not Custer needed the cube more than we do is still an arguable point, but then, no one had much use for Custer.

All evidence would indicate that the cube has no place in the modern world. Except for one thing. What do we have that Adam and Eve, the monkeys, the architect, and Custer did not have? The advertising agency. What else could convince over twenty million people to buy a cube?

2
You Can't Do the Cube

**AT LAST
THE SOLUTION
NO ONE
HAS BEEN WAITING FOR!**

The Perfect Way NOT To Do The Cube

CONSIDER THESE ADVANTAGES
OVER OTHER SOLUTIONS

1. You don't need to memorize moves!
2. Impossible to make mistakes!
3. Presents no complicated decision making!
4. Presents no decision making!
5. Not a gimmick!
   This is the real solution on how not to do the cube!
   Guaranteed not to work!

About The Author

Ernest N. Snively, a graduate from a prominent North Dakotan high school, felt that he had the necessary education to write this chapter. We weren't too sure he was right until we learned that he'd been an executive worker in the United States Postal Service for the last thirty years. "I've made it what it is today!" boasts Snively. He has done more than any other person to define the art of misplacing and delaying the delivery of mail. Considering the countless letters he's singlehandedly 'misdirected,' we found no reason why he'd have problems misplacing the paltry number of squares on the cube. We think that after reading his astute directions for *not* solving the cube, you will surely agree that he is an expert in this field.

YOU CAN'T DO THE CUBE!
By
Ernest N. Snively

About the Cube and Cube Solving

When you first got your cube it was in a finished condition; all six sides were a solid color. A few turns and twists and it looked like a bag of M & M's right? And you haven't been able to restore it to its original condition in all this time, have you? Well, don't worry about it. Forget it! It's like trying to put a broken egg back into shape. It *is* impossible. You can't do it! Once you understand and accept this important fact, you will have a lot more fun with your cube. Here at the Post Office we've all come to accept the fact that it's impossible to deliver the mail quickly and not lose packages, so we don't try be careful or to move quickly! We are all much happier with this attitude. And you can also be happy by applying this same attitude to your cube solving efforts. Simply direct your efforts towards impressing yourself and your friends as being *intelligent and knowledgeable* about all aspects of the cube and cube solving.

Use of Complex Terminology

The use of a complex, contrived and pedantic vocabulary is essential in my approach to not solving the cube. Why say "turn the blue and white side square to face the opposite direction", when you can almost as easily say: "Manually manipulate the blue square in such manner that it becomes juxtapositioned at a ninety degree angle to the adjoining white square (in compliance with OSHA safety parameters), and in such a manner that it will make a reversal of 180 degrees of itself in relation its relative positioning of the normative and accepted apportionment of the other squares!"

Isn't the latter wording much more exciting and authoritative? I can't quite figure out what it means, but when you say it while working the cube you will feel smart and your friends will perceive you as capable for the task.

Believe me, it works. How do you think I and all my friends ever reached high positions at the Postal Service? We simply admitted to our superiors that, no, we can't get the mail delivered properly, but we're at least doing it wrong in a very intelligent and educated manner. We knew they wouldn't want crass, uneducated (private) businessmen to take control of the System and do things less intelligently, even if they might do it faster, better and cheaper.

Likewise, your friends and yourself will be more impressed with your seemingly advanced intelligence than with the intelligence of the nine year old kid who claims to solve the cube in a matter of minutes. In cube solving, like in government, it is the credentials and the appearances that count, never the bottom line.

What is the Cubie's favorite hard science?
[Arcubology]

The Basic Solution

The Basic Solution to not solving the cube is so simple it's almost anti-climatic. Just turn the sides and corner pieces around at random. That's all! It works every time. You'll never solve it! It's foolproof! Oh sure, there's a 430 quintillion or something to one chance that you might accidently do it, but why worry about those odds? Why, you'd have a better chance of being fired from the Postal Service than you would of accidently solving the cube. Take it from me, you have no cause for worry.

What is the Cubie's least liked game of chance?
[Roulette]

Advanced Challenges

After several months of not solving the cube you'll probably be ready for additional challenges. I know I was. The best suggestion I can offer to you is that you attempt not solving the cube while engaged in some other activity. This can be quite challenging. I encourage all my fellow workers to play with the cube during work hours. Sure, it may slow things down a bit here in the office, but it does make everyone a lot happier. And being happy, both in cube solving and government working, is what it's all really about.

Don't ever give second thoughts to the end result.

3
The Thinking Person's Solution

The following is a complete transcript of a partial lecture given by the noted and sometimes controversial physicist, Dr. T.G. Bastian. Author of **The Twisting Wu Li Masters** and **N-Cube For The Millions.** The renowned octogenarian has now developed a foolproof method for solving the cube in **one** move. If you have difficulty following his instructions here, we suggest reading his handy illustrated booklet: "Deciphering Dimensions of the Bastian Approach."

Good evening fellow scientists and interested laypeople. I have been called by the university to present this lecture titled, "Multidimensional Time-Parity-Charge Relations of Modern Cube Solving." Normally, I would not deign to devote any of my limited time to such a commercialized, mundane child's toy, but there seems to be a matter of pleasing certain members of the Academy who have.... ah, but I digress. The sooner I get on with the lecture, the sooner we can all be finished.

What I hold in my hand is a scrambled cube. I confess, with some pride, that this is the first time I've actually held one, or even attempted to apply my universal theories to its solution. One purpose of this lecture, after all, is to demonstrate how an intelligent system of applied knowledge can quickly yield an immediate and correct solution.

To begin, this is a simple cube. Complete with six geometrically identical sides, it complies to all mathematical laws that govern such bodies. A casual further inspection reveals that each side contains nine moveable smaller cubes which can be rotated along three axes. Therefore, nine squares on six sides present 54 ways of organizing the cube. Also, since six of these smaller cubes can never change, there are but 48 different combinations possible to return the cube to its original isochromic six color condition. The problem seems simple enough. I fail to understand what all the fuss is about, since mathematically, one should be able to accomplish the feat of reorganizing the cube in less than six direct moves.

Let's now turn to the blackboard where I can graphically present the mathematical unity of this unique and colorful toy cube, (Draws a square) thus! This square represents the collected group of the cube's 54 combinatorial sides. You may envision it as a 4th-dimensional projection of a cube into our three dimensional world.

Imagine, if you will, that we were two-dimensional folks living there on the blackboard. Then, to us the cube would appear as a many-coloured area with some 54 different squares all compressed as a flat pancake. From this perspective, each time one would twist or rotate the cube, the colours would simply and mysteriously change for us. While in this two-dimensional world, we might be baffled and indeed its combinatorial possibilities would be to us infinite. Obviously, to understand and to solve the problem, we would have to leave the blackboard world and at least pretend to be in the third dimension to see it at least as someone folding six sheets of paper with as many colours.

Using this model then, the solution to the cube rests in defining an operand *R* from a 3-dimensional world into a bit more complex 4th-dimensional one. To accomplish this with ease, we must accept that the square drawn here on the blackboard is actually *the identical* presentation as is this representative of the same cube I now hold in my hands.

Let X represent the soon to be solved cube, and let each of the six sides be called S-1 to S-6. Each side, in turn, contains nine subsets which we can ignore since they are already held within the definition of each side. Other solutions, suggested by some other mathematicians lose their simplicity and elegance by confusing this most vital aspect of the cube. What we need to keep in mind is the goal that each of the six sides (S-1 to S-6) should *by definition* be made complete and properly oriented to their respective colors. This then, ends our geometric description of the cube. In case you fail to follow the logic, and I emphasize that you must, please refer to Quine's classic *Word and Object* for more detailed explanations.

Now for the easy part. Inspect the cube, and evaluate every case in which there is no obvious one-to-one Cantorian correspondence among the sides. For example, the cube that I now hold in my hand, has... 29 such discrepencies, or of the 54 possible combinations, more than half of them are correctly alligned. In other words, the ideal solution for this particular case will need only three or four turns of the cube, or a 50-50 chance of success in two turns.

What is the Cubie's favorite "school" of art?
[Cubism]

Of course, this analysis is based on our 4-Dimension projection of the cube under purely ideal conditions. Getting this to work in the real world, however, may be slightly more involved. So, let's begin by finding the one side that is more scrambled than any other, and hereafter refer to it as S-1. Likewise, we'll call the side closest to the proper solution S-6.

We aim to make S-1 perfect and it stands to reason that the other five sides will then fall into order by Dicherelet's Exclusion Principles. Remember, no side can ever have more than eight misplaced cubes, and since a statistically random cube will share its probability equally on all sides, no one side can be more confused than its neighbor. With this equation, we now have a valid starting point with which to exercise our minds and acquired scientific knowledge in regards to solving the cube. We needn't twirl it around in our hands like so many frustrated monkeys. For the purpose of visual proof of the solution, I shall now manipulate the cube in keeping with the successive steps of solution.

The first "fold" of the cube will align all the red squares of S-2 through S-5 to the S-1 side, leaving us with only five colors to work with. Thus! Now, we again scan the cube and find that only 8 squares remain out of order. Or, eight of the 54 remain incorrect. If we were to cut the cube in half, we would not have to continue this process. However, it seems that luck is in our favor, for one more "fold" will do the job.

Getting this last "Maxwellian Demon" back into its box is no small feat. It calls for higher levels of set theory application, since making the wrong dimensional-fold can result in steps that lead away from the solution. I think that a simple Markov Chain event simulation is best suited to the task.

Examine the Cube. Again take note of the worst side, which in this case is S-2, and solve the projected cube as though it were a seven-sided object. The hypothetical S-7 side, of course does not exist, but you can use it as the ultimate receiver of all misplaced colors. This is a radical departure from the traditional N-cube concept, since it does not require any formal mathematical training, and is commonly used by children who do not know anything about geometry or math.

So, the field of mis-aligned squares, are now all dumped into S-7. And by a simple extension to the real world, I merely turn the cube one more time... Thus! and Presto! The cube is completely solved.

Some of you are surely confused by this simple mathematical approach to solving the cube, and will now go out and attempt a similar solution with your cube. For that reason, I now open the lecture to any questions that you may have regarding the mechanics of applying my solution.

Q. What is the purpose of projecting the cube to the 4th dimension?

A. That's quite simple. You cannot "fold" a cube in this world. It's like trying to jam coins into a dollar change machine. It just won't work.

Q. I can see the Cantorian principles at work, but what do the Markov Chains have to do with it? Can't I just "fold" the cube a second time and get to the same place?

A. Not really. Its like folding the American flag, unless you first get rid of all the stripes, you'll never get the blue field and white stars correctly. I suggest that you read some Trudeau's *In Search of...* series, where the same principle is explained in simple language.

Q. I'm Doug Hofsitter from a prestigious midwestern college. Your solution is out of sight of my mind's eye, totally! First, how do you get off telling people that there are *only 54 possible combinations* to the cube when we all know that there are at least 5 quintatrillion ways to arrange the cube. And then, how did you do that in two moves? Even God's solution calls for seven moves.

A. Fine questions "Digger!" Your information channels seem confused by your fancy typesetting tricks and elaborate Escherian views. If I were selling books, I'd also tell everyone the largest numbers possible, but the facts remain: the cube *has* only six sides, and six colors. These are distributed by nine smaller squares, so, six times nine *is* 54! No more. No less.

As for the number of moves necessary, I guess I was just lucky. Sometimes it may take six moves — never more! Of course, if you like to twist the cube around, do so if it makes you feel better. But remember, anything more than six turns is an inefficient solution. Try it yourself... here, I'll scramble this cube up...(throws a curve to the rear of the hall).

Q. Does your explanation mean that if a Cube is projected to the 5th Dimension it can be solved by one turn?

A. Exactly! But to make it happen in our world, you must first "unfold" it once to the 4th, and then "fold" it six times to the 3rd dimension, so it may not always work.

Maybe an example will help. Imagine an ordinary railroad spike about the size of this microphone. If we project it into the 4th dimension, it would be a thick line; in the 5th dimension it would be a dot; and in the 6th dimension... well.., it would be something like Amtrack's Broadway Limited dumping its load at 65 mph along some desolate railroad crossing. In other words, each move to another dimension increases the possibilities, but delimits your analysis. So, I suggest that no cube solution should be done beyond the 4th dimension.

Q. I've got this cube that I still can't solve, and I don't understand a word you've said.

A. Your honesty is admirable. Try it this way. Pretend that your cube gets run over and flattened by a Mack truck. Now, put it back together by peeling the six sides apart and fold them each to make the final cube. Does that make sense to you? (Questioner nods an understanding smile).

Q. Someone poured Crazy Glue all over my scrambled cube. Can you help me solve it with your solution?

A. Immovable squares make any solution infinitely more complex. I'd suggest that you work it through a Reimean space. You know, by saddle-folding the edge squares atop each other. I'm certain that you'll find a solution with two or three extra steps. Personally, however, I'd focus my efforts to bring the solution into the real world. So, for example, if friends fail to see your solution, you might offer them some psylocybin, which can appreciably affect their perception of the solved cube.

Q. How many scrambled cubes are needed to find one that can be solved by one move?

A. That's simple! Since there are 54 combinations possible and each cube is identical after being solved; six scrambled cubes chosen at random will give you one that can be solved in one move, if I understand your question. To do this, project all six on top of each other in the 5th dimension. Now proceed to "unfold them" one at a time to the 4th. As you do this, you will find at least one cube that can be solved in one easy twist, according to Dicherlet's Principle.

Q. I've got a pet Schnauzer. He can solve the cube in less than 30 seconds. How does he do it?

A. That depends. Some domesticated armadillos have succeeded with the cube in less than 12.2 seconds, while household pets, being inbred, require more time. My guess is that your Schnauzer is an average household pet with possible dysfunctional/senility problems.

In general, the uncanny ability of many animals to successfully solve the cube suggests that they see the world in non-Eucledian terms, and have few problems of projecting objects into the 4th dimension. You might do well to study how your dog thinks.

If there are no further questions, we can now set aside our short-lived fascination with this amusing toy. If any of you are still confused and feel challenged by the cube, I encourage you to retire to your private spaces and ponder the mathematical principles we've discussed. I will gladly counsel you pertaining to our normal course work. By the suggestion of the Board of Examiners, our mathematics department will be using the scrambled cube as an Entrance Test. Specifically, such cubes will be given to all prospective students, who will be expected to solve the cube in under 12.2 seconds. With such standards, I doubt that we shall have any problems explaining advanced concepts and their application to an ever complex world. Hey! Digger! Have you solved it yet? (Growl of disgust echoes from the emptying Lecture Hall).

4
The Average Person's Solution

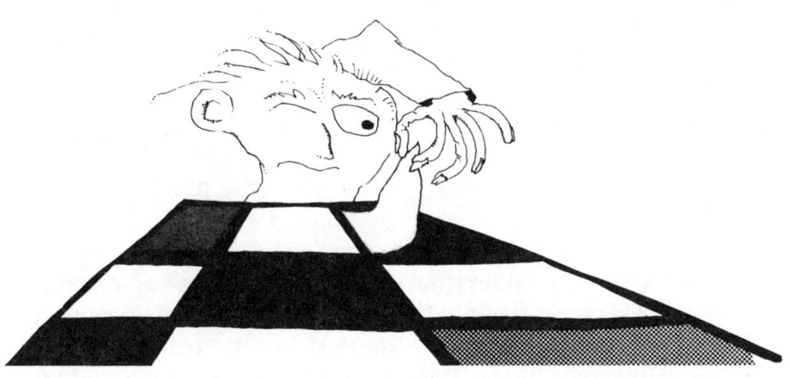

We hope you've enjoyed reading the previous chapters on how to solve the cube. No doubt they helped you immensely in your endeavors to solve the little puzzle. It's come to our attention, however, that not everyone is — how do we say this without suggesting insult? — is capable of following the otherwise lucid advice of cube solving experts.

Let's face it, most of you still can't solve the cube. No matter how many times the neighborhood genius shows you, no matter how many books you buy on the subject, no matter how many hours you invest in twirling, flipping and spinning the cube, you probably will never solve it. It's simply beyond your capabilities. Remember in high school, no matter how hard you tried; you never quite got a grasp on Algebra III; you never became fluent in the use of past perfect participles in in French, and you were never able to clearly define the difference between Plantaganets and Huegonots. And now, you can't solve the cube. What's worse, deep down inside, behind all the effort, beneath the piles of books guaranteeing a solution, you secretly know that you will never, ever succeed. Not now. Not ever.

Still, you look at that cube and you say to yourself, "Dear God in Heaven, give me the re-solve to solve!" Others, no doubt, quietly whisper in the dark corners of their lives, "Oh Satan, lord Beelzebulb, Demons of Darkness, I want something from you and you want something from me. Let's deal!"

There's really no need for you to go off the deep-end or make any deals with the Underworld. You've got us. And we've got the answer for you. Cheat.

Now please don't act shocked. Don't get self-righteous about something so obvious. We know that you've been thinking about it for quite some time and we're not here to argue with you over the ethics involved in this victimless crime. That's your problem. All we want to do is to provide you with the necessary information. If you do decide to cheat, you can do so with the full knowledge of all your available options.

Let's first consider the most popular form of cheating, namely, the repositioning of the colored square stickers on the surface of the cube. This is a method that is spoken of in near mythlike terms, like: "I've heard that some people actually peel the squares off..," or, "I have a friend who knew someone who...." It's parallel to the practice of varied and experimental sex — no one ever admits to actually doing it, but everyone seems to know an awful lot about it. They're not fooling us. (And don't ask us how we know.)

Although simple in concept, the peeling process is tricky, and a botched job can cause you great embarassment. We suggest that you first get as many squares as possible in the proper position, thus lowering the number that you'll have to swap. Now, with the aid of a razor blade, carefully lift the unmatched squares and put them in their proper place. Avoid touching the sticky substance on the back of the plastic squares, or it can lose some of it's ability to stick.

If someone spots a sloppy job (torn squares, loose edges, uneven alignment) and dares to accuse you of cheating, you will be disgraced and lose face. Be neat. Take your time. On the other hand, you might turn the table and ask your accusers how they happen to know what a cheat job looks like.

For a quick, slop job of cheating that is passable only at a distance, try spray enamel paint. You'll need six cans, one to match each of the six colors on the cube. Carefully die cut a stencil to match the pattern of the squares and spray away. Up close, it may look tacky, but this approach usually works in a pinch.

Another common form of cheating is to dismantle the cube and then reassemble the parts in a finished condition. Your greatest risk is possibly breaking some of the plastic pieces. Keep a tube of super-glue handy for this event.

Many frustrated Cubies 'service' their cubes by, "...taking them apart, cleaning and lubricating the parts". Naturally, the cube is put back together in a finished — solved condition. The faster you can service your cube, the quicker you can solve it. So, practice growling and complaining that the cube doesn't "feel right"; giving you opportunity to sneak away to service it.

Many people hesitate in taking the cube apart, owing to a spurious myth that has circulated for some time, namely, that a cube can be incorrectly reassembled, making it forever unsolvable! Balderdash! There is no such thing as an unsolvable cube! This folklore is further promoted to provide some feeble excuse for those who would cheat. Don't fool yourself. Take pride in your cheating for what it is. Go ahead! Take screwdriver in hand and make that damn cube right again.

The most advanced form of cheating involves some deft sleight of hand. For some, this can be more challenging than actually solving the cube. To do the trick you'll need a scrambled, unsolved cube and a second new one in it's original, solved condition. Also, you should wear a loose, long sleeved shirt or better yet an oversized sports jacket.

While seemingly attempting to solve the scrambled cube, with your back turned, secretly exchange it for the solved one that's hidden in your sleeve. Presto digitalis, eh? There are two important points to remember. One, remember that old stage magic maxim to never perform the same trick twice in one evening. Two, don't let anyone scramble your solved cube!

These are the basic forms of cube cheating. Experiment with them and see which one works best for you. Remember to take pride in your ability to cheat successfully. It's nothing to be embarrassed about. Some people can solve cubes, some can cheat. We should each fulfill our own unique niche in life.

5
Holistic Cubie

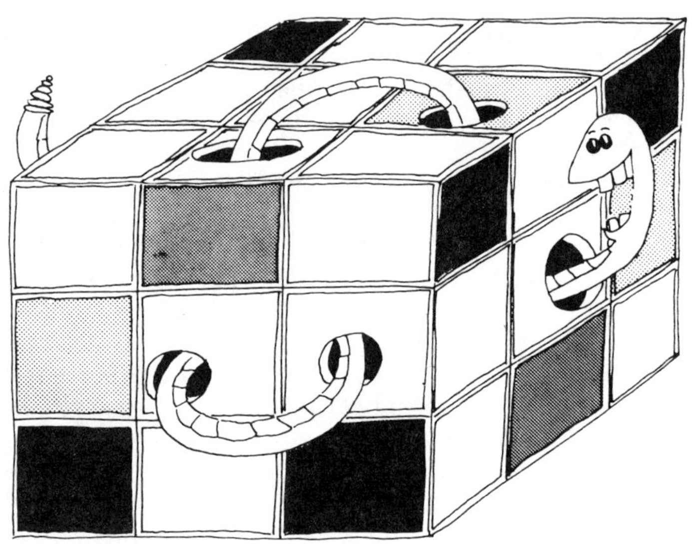

Dear Authors, Editors and Publisher,

It's a peak-experience to write you. I mean, it's like taking part in the building of Atlantis. Imagine having these thoughts transmitted to future historians and cubeologists. I'm sure, totally, that they'll try to explain The Cube as some mystical or religious artifact and like how it was used to lead a world-wide Cubie Revolution. My writing you is far-out, for sure, and you'll do the future alot of good by publishing your book.

Why not use my letter in your fun-filled handbook? It'll help to tell people how good Cubing really is. Besides, I'd help you sell your book to the Universal Cube Club, all 8,254,991 members. Well, it's not really organized yet, but I'm getting it together, for sure. When I first saw the full-page announcement of your book in *Total Cubing* magazine — it freaked me out! I mean, totally. Like who would want to win a first prize to go on an all-expense-paid trip to the Himalayas with Lawrence Welk, the Osmonds, and a real Taiwan Cube manufacturer? That's squeeky! I mean, really grilled! Who would want part of meeting all those Zen monks anyway? They'll just paw the Cube, become fascinated by its pretty colors and then predict some bizarre, cosmic things. They won't 'unscramble' it! But for sure they'll do the Cube right and make it fit into bigger universal things.

You're probably wondering who I am. Well, let me introduce myself. I'm the long arm of all those Cube owners who can't solve the Cube. I'm one of the twenty million hands that twist, flip, and rotate the Cube without success and still get a charge from it. We're the hands of a world that toils for the chance to make the Cube's rainbow colors dance. Just as Sagan and Watts say, we're being at one with the "whole cosmos;" where there is no I, nor you. Like, after all, we're all spiritual Cubies from the heart of the universe. Everything is part of the Great Cube.

Take the stars for instance. We've thought them round, but it's really neat to think of them as cubes that only look round to us because they're far-out, or some Doppler red-blues of space make their edges fade away. Every night, stars come and go; each moving in an infinite combination; just like the Cube. The stars, their planets and moons could all be giant corner squares of the whole universe. That's why celestial bodies are always in the right place, not like spokes in a wheel, but like parts of a big box that rotates, flips and turns to create our seasons and keep us all alive. They've always been far-out and full of color.

The whole universe could certainly be a giant Cube — but its not straight at the edges. It never was. Space is the place where all cubes are, and space itself is squiggly and curved. So, that's another obvious reason why the corner squares get twisted back into themselves as on some giant Mobius Belt. That's why we never can see the actual corners. It also makes sense that in a Cube universe our lives will always get twisted around; like a Kafkan play with bribing beads at a Hessian trial!

You see, we're all a part of the universal Cubie soul. We sit daily on a fifty-yard-line of a Giant Cubie Bowl, each of us busy flipping our Cube. Take sports, for instance, I might cheer Jimmy Conners while you cheer for Dr. "J" or George Bush. Yet, they're all part of the game and we all make colorful plays on insufferable squares of a flat, dull politico/sporting plane. It's inescapable, we're all rooting for big-game players who've made Cubing the greatest American participant sport. It's especially noticeable when we strike for more money, vote for more taxes, get unemployed, or prevent a nuclear war. Hooray to any sport that helps Cubing.

Let's face it. The Cube has already changed the way we think. Like, for example, I knew this teacher who always got freaked out when anyone compared red apples to oranges. What a bummer! He'd call it "equivocation," or something. But today, with all the electronic game stuff, things are alot cooler. Like no one, but no one, comes down on you for comparing a Cube with some other Cube, yet they're just about as different!

Years ago, a Cube was just another Cube. Then we found the moving colors and made them "personal cubes", to be twisted, turned, admired and analyzed. Today, since we see the Cube everywhere, the Cube has once more become "just such a Cube." It's again nothing special. A part of this awakening is that we can now take Cube in hand and turn the colors for sheer enjoyment. The Cube is always perfect, no matter where its colors are.

Making fun, or ridiculing anything about the Cube is little different than standing in awe of its great shadow. After all, that too is part of its Zen. And, like it or not, we are all part of it. *Tse-juggling* has long been a Cubbhism discipline which rides an edge between its ridicule and exploring its inspirational mysteries. Its students practice the *I-Pass* (Tossing of The Cube) to predict the future.

In highlighting our inabilities to control the Cube, followers of the *I-Pass* have given its celebration great communal and societal value; especially in teaching the ways to "speak in Cubes." This development of Cubbhism uses *CUBIC* as the ultimate universal language. Unlike the common spoken word, CUBIC uses no tense, syntax, or cumbersome; punctuations! With it we all can say just what we meant, and mean only what we say. It's been compared to communicating with neighbors over a backyard fence, but only "five inches under the ground," as Yamaha the renowned *I-Pass* master once remarked.

To learn CUBIC, one can follow The Way of Cube (Chetwixt) and to always expect the unexpected. It's origin is based on a parallelism in history, something analogous to the first Cube springing from the mind of a wild Hungarian to infest the Earth; the CUBIC language is destined to emerge from Earth to spread throughout the universe. It is accepted that any alien space visitor, cumfy within its UFO can tell at a glance our full intellectual and cultural level of evolution by the use of CUBIC through the Cube's color combinations. It is perfect mathematics and a ready-to-use universal language. So if CUBIC can be understood by someone who has never set foot on Earth, it should be relatively easy for all of us to learn.

Gnome Chumski's CUBIC Dictionary tells how, for example, Red-Red-Red on the Yellow-side means: "How's your work going?" While, Green-Yellow-Blue on the Red-side means: "Hold the ketchup. Heavy on the mustard". Billions upon billions of such combinations are possible. And with it comes an endless opportunity for puns, inuendoes, and poetry.

Through CUBIC this letter to you reads: Red-Yellow-Green, Yellow-Blue-White, Orange-Green-Green, (the last Green is there for humor sake!). You see, the Cube is not simply a chunk of cheap plastic stickered with primary colors; rather, it is an intelligent entity, just as a river, a rainbow or an old shop rag used to soak up spilled hydraulic fluid. The Cube is all those things and much much more.

Medical science tells us that 'solving' the Cube takes less than 10% of our total brain's ability. Great mathematicians or cubologists use less than that amount. So, if solving the cube is that easy, you may as well use the other 90%; move on to another level of cubing.

Of course, there are those who scoff at your mathematical shallowness or call your quest for Zen a mere 'cover-up,' for ineptness. These critics are unenlightened boo's who are stuck in a technical pit with the Cube. It is the wiser who accepts an inevitablity of failure, and then laughs in the face of the inescapable. The Cube is multi-tracked in its complexity and its elegant nature is all around us; no wind, no threat of famine, or pestilance can stop its appointed rounds!

Szepseg, the Beauty of the Cube, is a 2nd step in the Tao of the Cube. This tells how its "suchness" makes Cubes look attractive to us all. I'm especially referring to the insides of the Cube. The part that makes it a whole-cube. It's very soul; the beauty beneath the outside color stickers.

Once Erno, a renowned Zen Cube master, told his students to remove all the stickers from their Cubes and scramble the sides. One student asked: "But Master, how can we then know its proper solution?" to which the learned sage replied: "We must each turn to our best side." The student was then hit on the head with his Cube and told to take up arc welding.

To find this "best side" we first turn-in on the Cube's perfect geometry. We look at the smaller cubes that make the whole. Their one-to-one relation to the other elevates each individual mini-cube's to an "unconscious collective," as Master Levy-Strauss once called it in telling the mysteries of the Blue Cube. Every cube finds its own purpose and its own indentity. Still, every cube seeks its truth from a different standpoint each time we flip its sides. This then is the meaning of 'szepseg'. Through it one honors the center cube about which the other cubes move. We also come to accept the less fortunate corner cubes who are forever lost in chasms of negative space. None of the cubes is truly better, as all cubes share a common element and rest with strangers in the night while we, the Cube solvers meditate our next move.

Once we can accept that all parts of the Cube are "nothing special," we can find the key to the *No-Cube*; or, how "solving" the cube is just as impossible as getting a Big Mac sandwich back into the cow.

Unfortunately, the world today is much divided about how to best work the Cube. One school advocates total in-volvement in-to the In-ner Cube, of our in-ner thoughts; while the other simply doesn't seem to give a damn. In our pluralistic world it is no simple task to idenitfy who's who, yet as a rule of thumb, Eastern Cubbhists work *with* the cube; while latter Western Cubies tend to work *on it.*. Both realize that the Cube is always changing. One accepts it, while the other tries to force it to change.

Eastern ways of the Cube call for open hands, used to turn its sides and praise the Cube's mysteries. In contrast, solemn Western approaches to the Cube often use a clenched fist by which attempts are made to beat the Cube into submission. The method you choose depends entirely on your **Khubba,** or, "how you cube."

Each of us has a different Khubba that leads us to how we relate with the Cube. Confusions over this basic concept have led some wise scholars and technicians to misuse the Cube. Some have taken Khubba to mean "predestined failure" leading them to long hours of torment, broken fingernails and sprained wrists. Sadly, these folks miss-out from the good Khubba powers held in the Cube; in its stead they find the creation of bad vibes or mis-vented hostilities. Good Khubba, on the other side, leads to universal harmony and communion with the Great Cube. These bring joy and inner-peace to both the Cube and its user.

One's interacting with the Cube is not unlike watching television. It all depends on the channel you flip to. On a bad night, or, in the hands of the misguided, the Cube may lead one to sheer hell, no less than any sitcom or "Green Acres" rerun ever known. I have personally treated victims of "bad Cubing" in emergency wards for bloodied hands, lacerated arms and legs, and even a case of blinding from an airborne Cube that was hurled in anger at an innocent heckler. Indeed, unless you treat the Cube with reverence and care, the consequences can be unthinkable.

For me it is obvious that the Cube is something to work **with,** rather than to work **on.** Before interfacing with it however, you should set all wants and desires to rest; approach the Cube without any hidden motives to its 'proper' solution. In my search to find the truth within the Inner Cube, I've often found new, sometimes strange lands of thought, by simply not imposing my will upon it. Only last night I learned something remarkable about the Cube. You see, my landlord Irv always comes by at the end of the month for his money. So yesterday, while deep in meditation with my Cube to find a Blue/Green connection, I was interrupted by his pounding on my front door. "Hey Bum! Howzabout the rent? If you don't pay me by tomorrow noon, you'll be out on the street!"

The month before, I showed Irv how to solve his Cube, but apparently he didn't think the lesson worth enough for another month's rent. But he did re-decorate the apartment building to resemble a Cube and then to 'color-key' each tenant. My door had the big red square stickered on it. Irv has a strange sense of humor. Anyway, the whole event made me see the Cube as a giant warehouse of information. For example, Shakespeare's entire works can be placed into one of its corner edges! I tried explaining that to Irv, but he got spun-out. Well, to make the story brief, I'm writing this letter from a local Burger Chef, thinking about how I can get my stuff (including my 93 cube pyramid collection) out of the basement of the apartment building.

Not having a Cube is no reason for not using it. For real, I no longer need a *physical* Cube to practice its Zen. After all, the Cube is only a crude visual-aide to see its true form. Like I can simply create a Cube in my mind. I start with a square and do it six times. There! Now I'll just scramble it and use my mind's eye to see it in different directions. There! Look, I'm sure! That one yellow/green cube can tell me exactly what you're now thinking. That's right! I can use the Cube to see exactly what you're thinking right now! This is Cube-ESP, and its like a total Cube experience! By turning the Cube slowly — at 1 degree per minute, I can also tell the future (or the past). This is "Rolling Out the Cube" and it makes the Cube a psychic lens into people's thoughts. With Cube-ESP I can see what you're thinking about all the time — like from where you started reading this sentence, and probably how far you'll keep reading.

Rolling Out is an art that can reveal some things best left unsaid. Like grim visions of slimy, muddy, snapping turtles chomping their way through an emergency computer cable at a SAC command base in central Florida. Wow! I think that just happened! I'm sure. You better check it out! I'll bet the media won't report it though. You see, Rolling Out can get brill, so I'll stop before ugly things start happening, (like a 9 megaton Trident missfires, or the bowels of Hell springing open to suck-out our life energy as a vaccuum cleaner to bone marrow). Thinkies like these are too cosmic for most Cubies to face.

By now you're surely wondering why I bother to tell you all these fun thoughts about the Cube. Well, the Cube is such a wonderful event, and that's it. Believe me, no *real* Zen Cube master would waste away the time to tell anyone about the Cube, but I'm still ego-bound and frankly very bored of sitting here on a cold street with a sign: "I Solve Cubes For A

Nickel.'' I do this thing only for coffee and pocket money while reconsidering my career at the ad agency. Imagine, I actually turned down the Cube account in 1979! I called it a "stupid Hunkie toy that wouldn't sell." Later, I flipped out. Totally.

Before giving up the Cube, I must tell you about all those techno Cube and computer game books. I mean, like they're really stupid. They're all the same. They've got no human-ness in them. Most are like blueprints to some nuclear power plant or an operations manual for a bulldozer. They only tell you how to *do the cube* but never tell you why you *should*. After all, a scrambled Cube or lost Pac-Man game is also of great value.

A nice relaxed way to relate with the Cube is to drink some Rosehip tea and sit in a lotus posture. First, reverently hold the cube in your open hands, but before turning anything, say ''Hello!'' to it. Touch it gently on all sides and inspect its alignment. Are the stickers on crooked? Has anyone switched colors on the Cube lately? Are all six colors there? (There should be nine little cubes for each color). Once you get comfortable with the cube and can no longer tell its temperature from yours, think about turning one of its faces. Don't do it yet; just think about it.

Now consider its six sides, each has its own unique color and the whole Cube is made of 57 seperate, but joined individual entities. These baby cubes were each at once ''home'', sitting undisturbed and not bothering anyone. Then one day, as though attacked by a horde of Eastern Tartars, they were ripped from their peaceful wombs and scattered throughout the cube's universe of a multibillion combinations. They now shriek and call out to you for salvation and their fate is in your humble hands. Only you, here and now, can restore order to an otherwise chaos ridden world as presented by the scrabbled Cube. This is no small responsibility; rather it is a moral imperative of no lesser consequence than the Gettysburg Address or opening a can of warm Spam on a hot July Sunday afternoon.

Before you move any of the sides, align your body direction to everything else. I usually like to face Polaris or True North because the Cubie Ether Wind (CEW) blows always from the South. You'll find this wind of great help, especially in moving the yellow cubes to their home side.

Close your eyes, chant a Cubbha Mantra, like 'blu-blu-blu' and now gently turn the Cube in a direction that feels most comfortable. Allow the inner-vision of its faces to guide your way, and as you approach a correct combination of turns, the Cube will tell you how to go. At times it may also release a warm colorful aura — a brilliant radiation that tells you that it and you are at one with everything in the universe.

At times you may be tempted to stop and evaluate your progress, or to see the Cube as it 'really is'. Don't become impatient, for what your eyes see can deceive your ultimate goal for union with the Cube. Especially be aware of analytic thoughts as they will mislead you. For example, if you see a particular side getting 'closer', you're being deceived, for sure. This is known as *Bada-Cubbha*, the 'Cube-Fool', whereby the Cube tests your sincerity and can trick novices into a belief that a 'solution' is at hand. Diplomats and Zen Cube masters know of this false security, which calls for the *ta-ta* view, or the total and complete dismissal of anything seen or heard. To practice ta-ta, close your eyes and continue twisting the Cube until you again feel at one with it. Remember, the problem is never in the Cube — you carry the problem to the Cube.

Another ta-ta is the reach to the elusive "Seventh Side" of the Cube. This comes about as you think of how the cube once was, and then imagine how it may look again someday when all the colors will match the six sides. To find this state with the Cube, choose an unseen color, like Skyblue Pink, or Banana Blue, and imagine the primary colors to fall into their proper places on the Cube. Japanese Cubbhatori sees this as a sudden geomeric happening, as though the seventh side leaps out at the seeker; but I tend to think of it as the never-found seventh color. It's like blue turtle soup, green rubies, or the black crystals of Thomas Mann's joyful tale of a small boy in "Snow." Each non-color you see can enrich your relation in being at one with the Cube.

So, that's about it. Once you hitch a ride on the Cubic Ether Wind, you'll travel, smiling along in the gentle art of Zen Cubing. You can be loose on the world with ease and inner tranquility. But remember, the Cube is only a tool at best. It is merely spatial and temporal, and as such it can lure you into thinking about it. Whenever this urge happens to you, you must learn to let go. Never cling to the Cube. Release all your fixation with it. Tell others about its wonders and then step aside while they get involved. See how the "suchness" of the Cube affects their lives and imagine a Cubeless Universe. Learn to live on the Seventh Side, and that's Cube Satori.

Sincerely,

Baba Rama Cubik

6
The Great Debate

THE QUESTION:

Is the Cube destructive to the American Way of Life?
and
Should it be outlawed?

THE DEBATERS:

Pro — The Right Reverend Squary Foolwell
Con — Cubeboy Publisher Hugh Cubener

OPPOSED
An Opinion by Hugh Cubener

"To be perfectly honest, I really don't understand what the problem is. The cube is not destructive to the American way of life — it *is* the American way of life! As such, there's no rational reason for making it illegal for consenting adults — and minors — to freely take part in the joyous act of cubing. To take the cube away from Americans is to take away the very essence of America — that free wheeling, colorful, constantly changing, complex yet simple character that epitomizes modern, liberated life.

"As owner and publisher of *Cubeboy* magazine, I've tried to expound on the mature, intelligent way of thinking that most freedom loving and responsible Americans adhere to. The Cubeboy Philosophy, quite simply, is 'if it feels good, do it!'. Now, this is not a license to violate the rights of others, but a liberty to practice life as one wishes. If one wishes to practice cubing, as I myself do, it's one's own business, not the business of Reverend Squary Falwell.

"I personally urge all Americans to practice cubing. It has no dangerous side effects, costs very little, and is a lot of fun. It'll improve your entire outlook on life.

"If more people were to try cubing, they'd be very surprised. They'd certainly have to agree with me that the cube is neither destructive to the American way of life, nor should it be outlawed.

"I'd like to personally invite the Reverend Squary to the Cubeboy Mansion in Chicubo. There, he can partake in a variety of cubing alternatives. He can cube with any combination of colors and practice any patterns he wishes. He can use either a private room complete with sauna and strategically placed mirrors, or he can use the communal cubing room where other cubies might watch or join in with him. He can even use two cubes at once, if he's into that sort of thing. No need to be embarrassed here, Squary. 'If it feels good, do it!.'"

AGREED
An Opinion by the Reverend Squary Foolwell

"It grieves me to hear that there are men who confuse destruction with life. For the American passion with the cube is not life, in fact, it is anti-life. It is wanton the destruction of life. To practice a simple mental exercise is one thing — to let the desire to solve the cube become an obsession is quite another.

"Now, despite publicity to the contrary, I pride myself in being a liberal man. I would like to let all men choose their paths freely, but I must persevere in my efforts to outlaw the cube. The normal individual does not have the necessary strength to resist its obsession. The cube is much like the addictive drug — once man has tasted it, he can never get enough. And for those who have seen and solved the mystery of the cube, their only goal in life is to be able to solve it faster and faster. For them, sadly, it can never be solved fast enough.

"So far, I have spoken only of the immediate victims of cubing. But there are others; friends, relatives and acquaintances of the hardcore cubie. They must suffer, also. They must watch the slow and inevitable decay of a loved one. Is this right? Should it be permitted when it can easily be prevented? I think not.

"There is also one other matter which should be discussed, and which Mr. Cubener, as a businessman, should appreciate. Millions of work hours are lost every day because of the working man's efforts to solve the cube. Worker productivity is down for the seventh month in a row. The cause — the cube. And less people are out in the stores buying products. They're busy at home trying to solve the cube. I needn't discuss what has happened to church attendance figures. I ask you, what could be more characteristic of the American way of life than producing and consuming? Yet these are the very qualities of life that the cube is slowly destroying. The cube, I'm sure you'll agree, must be outlawed.

"We may have failed in these present state and national legislative sessions to accomplish our goal, but we'll be back. This is an issue which just will not go away."

7
The Cubie Health Plan

There is a popular misconception afoot that the cube is to be used only for intellectual stimulation. This is simply not so. The versatile cube can be used to improve you physical condition as well as your mind. No doubt your fingers and wrists are in peak physical condition as a result of thousands of hours of traditional cubing, but what about the rest of your body? If you've been sitting around playing with the cube, it no doubt needs some serious attention. In this chapter, we offer a complete Cubie Health Plan. It covers exercise, diet and all around well-being.

AEROBIC CUBING

By now, everyone is aware of the value of aerobic exercise. It is defined as exercise that increases the heart rate and makes the blood pump faster. (Incidentally, increased blood pressure resulting from cube-solving frustration does not count as a form of aerobic exercise!) This popular form of exercise can easily be done with the aid of one's cube. You might want to try the following exercises:

Cube Pick-Up: place cube on the floor, stand with knees straight, bend over, pick up cube, stand up and twist to the right and then to the left. Bend over and put the cube back on the floor. Repeat 20 times (even if you do reach a solution before that time.)

Cube Sit-Up: with your knees bent, hold the cube between them and do 20 sit-ups, making sure your forehead touches the cube each time.

RUNNING AND CUBING

Of course, *everyone* is into jogging, but it can be so tedious and boring! So why not kill two birds with one stone and cube while you jog? The cubing will take your mind off jogging, or vice versa, depending on which of the two is your least favorite activity. If you're one of the more "in tune" joggers who likes to listen to music while jogging, try some inspirational tunes on the order of "Twisting the Night Away." For those runners with endurance and competitive streaks, consider the possibilities of cross country cubing. Not only would the winner have to finish the race first, he'd have to finish the cube before anyone else!

CUBE-RELATED TENSION RELEASE

If you've been cubing in vain and have yet to solve the little bugger, we've got the perfect exercise for you. The 'tension releaser' will not only remove that mental frustration from your mind, it'll put your body into better physical condition. Our favorite is to repeatedly throw a cube against a brick wall. We don't mean half-heartedly, either. You have to get the old blood pumping fast and furious.

There's a wide variety of tension releasing exercises you can pursue. How about 'kick the cube', a throwback to childhood days? Or a session of batting practice, an hour of teeing off at the driving range, or an afternoon of slam dunking? One exercise that is popular with the elite cubie is squash.

WATER SPORTS

If swimming is your sport, how about diving for cubes? We understand this is gaining rapidly in popularity in some Mexican resorts where the locals would dive off high cliffs for coins.

You might also try improving your lung capacity by working the cube underwater. Can you solve it before you have to come up for air? Exercise caution against hyperventilation and hypertension! (See the *L.L. Cube Catalogue* for the rust proof cube designed for water sports.)

HEAVY STUFF

If you're one of those cubies who likes to hang out at Muscle Beach or lift weights at the local spa, you're going to love "pumping cube". This involves some slight modification of the cube. Simply drill a hole in each cube and fill with wet cement. Let it dry and — Presto! Instant weights. Of course, this does render traditional cubing virtually impossible, but if you're into muscle building you'll probably get more use (and enjoyment) out of your cube than ever before.

ISOMETRICS

For those of you interested in anaerobic exercises — a series of muscle exertions and relaxations — your cube can be a great aid. Instead of using door jambs and the backs of chairs, do your pushing in and pulling apart on a cube! Many cubies don't know it, but they are already practicing isometrics when attempting to solve cubes. They can be seen pushing and pulling with great vigor, muttering: "Move! Move! Over here!

We hope that our list of exercises provides an option for all cubies, the ardent athlete and the weekend recreationalist alike.

Incidentally, we understand there is a movement stirring to organize Olympic Cubing. We think it's admirable that competitive cubies everywhere want to design other forms of competition beyond the old "beat the clock" contests at the local shopping malls.

NUTRITION AND DIETING

Along with every good program of exercise goes the need for good eating habits. For the ardent cubie, only a specialized diet will suffice. For most people our Back To Basics diet will work fine. This diet requires that you eat at least one square meal per day. Our Radical Diet, for those who are desperate to lose weight, and have the willpower to match the desperation, requires that you eat only when you have successfully completed the cube. Your eventual weight loss will be dependent upon your solving skills.

The silliest and most fun filled diet we offer is the Color Diet. On this diet you can only eat foods that match a color on the cube, with a different color for every day of the week (you can take Sundays off). On Monday, for example, eat only orange colored food; carrots, pumpkins and tangerines. On Tuesday, eat only yellows; bananas, corn and grapefruit. We reserve the color blue for Fridays. Not having found any blue foods, we fast on that day.

A final note: Before embarking on any radical change of exercise or diet, consult your doctor.

8
The L.L. Cube Catalog

Are you going in circles trying to find the perfect gift for the cubie in your life? Then search no further. Our new catalog offers you a wide selection of exciting new products guaranteed to delight any cube fanatic. There's something in here for everyone!

CUBE PEDESTAL

A must for all cube owner. This distinctive chrome-plated pedestal, in a choice of two colors, makes an ideal storage place for a cube when not in use. A great addition to the coffee table, too!

Silver colored chrome $20.95
Gold colored chrome $25.95

MAINTENANCE KIT

A handy vinyl case contains everything you need to keep your cube operating smoothly and looking like new. Kit includes a specially formulated lubricant for easier twirling and flipping, a mild cleanser for removing those offensive smudges, and a unique new polish to give those squares a special shine. Order now and receive FREE our own polishing cloth of 50% flannel fabric.

Basic Brown Vinyl Case $8.95
Deluxe Black Leatherette $11.95

BASIC ZIPPERED CUBE CARRYING CASE

A versatile and attractive bag of water repellent nylon for handy cube transportation. Piped with attractive contrasting color, comfortable webbed shoulder strap, and plastic lined. Two compartments. Handsome, yet durable.

Red with Blue $6.25
Green with Blue $6.25
Red with Green $6.55

DIGITAL CUBE ALARM CLOCK

Are you into timing your cube solving? This custom crafted digital clock in cube disguise is just what you need. Folds into it's own traveling case. Colorful, good looking, and should last a lifetime!

Clock with Beeper $45.00 Clock with Musical Alarm $52.50

MINI-COMPUTER FOR CUBING

If cube solving taxes your brain, let our computer give you a hand. Color coded and programmed specifically for cubing, our little wizard won't give you the answer but will give you some help with memory storage problems your brain can't handle. Hi-Tech!

Quartz-LED Display $130.00
Deluxe Computer with Printout .. $240.00

SURE-GRIP GLOVES

For the purist cubie. These lightweight gloves made of a supple silk and knit fabric hug your hands and give a greater feeling of control when cubing. Specify size.

Tan or Grey $18.00

MAGNETIC CUBES

The perfect gift for the traveling salesman in your family. A rugged design that attaches to the dashboard for easy access. Always have a cube at your fingertips!

3" x 3" (for compacts) $9.00
4½" x 4½" (for luxury cars) $13.00

FLOATING CUBE

High quality rubber makes this cube ideal for those into water sports. You'll never be without your cube again. Can't sink, rust or deflate. Also functions as a life preserver in deep water emergencies. Rope included.

Child's Cube $14.95
Adult's Cube $24.95

The "PREPPIE CUBE"

Just your average cube done completely in shades of pink and green.

Preppie Cube $12.50

DESIGNER CUBES

If fashion is the name of your game, these top name designer çubes will suit you to a 'T'. Fashion's biggests were selected to contribute to this year's line. If status is what you seek in your cubing, look no further.

The Gloria Vandervilt Cube — Pastels Plus

The Gucci Cube — A 'G' on every square

The Bill Blast Cube — Distinctly Masculine

The Channel Cube — Very French, mon cher!

You'll be billed upon delivery. The price? If you have to ask, you can't afford it.

ICE CUBES

Having a cube party? What better addition to the festivities than cube shaped ice cubes? Specially shaped trays and food coloring can turn your dull drinks into great conversation pieces. What a way to "break the ice!"

Ice CUBE Tray & Coloring $6.50
Additional Trays................... $4.50

PLASTIC DINNERWARE

Throw tradition to the wind with a new concept in food service. Plates and cups designed in cube motif. All six colors of the cube are used in these sturdy, non-breakable plastic dishes. Mix 'n' Match to your hearts content! Serve square meals for fun!

16 Piece Dinnerware Set.......... $29.95

COMPLETE LINE OF LINENS

To compliment your home's cube decor, you can choose from our wide and complete selection of cube inspired linens. Tablecloths, napkins, kitchen linens, even linens for the bedroom and bath are included. Three patterns to choose from. For details, consult the special loose leaf appendix. Now!

CUBIE WATERBED

Our most handsome piece of furniture is this rosewood waterbed. Perfect for resting after a hard day's cubing. Bookcase headrest has special compartments for cubes, your Mini-Computer and other cube accessories. This bed will do any cube fan proud when topped off with our fine cube linens and granny 'square' blanket.

Complete Waterbed, 80"x80" $450.00

THE CUBE WEDDING

Are you getting married to a true blue cubie? Then we have the ideal guide for planning your wedding with a cube theme. Our new boo, "Tying the Old Square Knot" has oodles of handy suggestions, such as planning square dances for the wedding reception, honeymoon opportunities in Cuba and more! This in only a sampling of the helpful hints you'll find in our wedding guide. And by all means, don't forget the sugar cubes!

Tying the Old Square Knot (paperback). $4.95

LINGERIE

To complete your wedding trousseau, Freddie's of Hollywood has designed a complete line of cube inspired lingerie exclusively for our customers. You'll twirl and flip! Especially at the sight of the lingerie with the strategic squares missing and the... well, you'll have to order the catalog to find out. For sale to cubies over 21 only!

Freddie's Cube Lingerie Catalog... $1.00

9
Squaring Off

SQUARING OFF: A Debate Between Supply Side Cubist David Blockman and Senate Cube Control Sub-Committee Chairman, Jacube Javitts. (The following is a transcript of a nationally televised program.)

Narrator: Welcome, viewers, to today's debate on SQUARING OFF. The Federal Government of the United States has for some time been aware of the unconscionable existence of the condition of the national cube. Tremendous inequalities exist. No one side has nine squares of the same color. In the last fifty years the Federal Government has taken drastic measures to correct this situation, all to little apparent avail. The American public, dissatisfied with the results, voted overwhelmingly in the last election to try a different approach to the grave problem. This new approach is known as Supply Side Cubism. From the President's Administration, we have with us the chief advocate of Supply Side Cubism, David Blockman.

What is a Cubie's least favorite form of intermediation?
[The Round Table Discussion]

Blockman: Thank you, I'm glad to be here.

Narrator: Also with us, is a strident critic of supply side cubism, Senator Jacube Javitts.

Jacube: Call me Jacube, please. I'm a man of the people and would like to be addressed as such.

Narrator: Very well. Gentlemen, let's begin to debate on the question, "Is Supply Side Cubism A Viable Approach For Restoring The National Cube?" an opening statement by Mr. Blockman, please.

Blockman: Certainly. The basic idea behind Supply Side Cubism is that the six sides of the cube, pursuing their own self interests, will quickly and efficiently work towards achieving their own desires. That is to say, each side will be a solid nine squares of the same color, thus solving the problem of the national cube. To facilitate the process of Supply Side Cubism, my office has and will continue to remove inhibitive government regulations and excessive taxation.

Narrator: Thank you, Mr. Blockman. Jacube, if you will.

Jacube: Mr. Blockman's thinking is exactly the reason why the Federal Government became involved in — and should continue to be involved in — regulation of the cube. His laissez-faire attitude is what led to the Great Mix-Up of 1929 — and who alive today can ever forget that disastrous Rainbow Friday. Those events were the direct result of having no realistic regulation of the cube or....

Blockman: If you'll excuse me — the Great Mix-Up came about because of the Federal Government's intervention in the movement of the cube. The government guaranteed a security to the cube — that colors could be quickly returned to their proper positions. This was a promise it couldn't deliver on. The cube didn't know it at the time — it operated with a false sense of security. Sides invested colors indiscriminately all over the cube banking on future returns that the government guaranteed. When it became apparent what was happening, the sides panicked. They spun, twirled and flipped until no one knew where anything was. Some colors didn't even remember which side was theirs. Had the government made no promises, there'd never have been a problem and we wouldn't be squaring off today.

Jacube: Am I to assume, Mr. Blockman, that you'd have us return to the days of the Robber Squarens! When one side would get all of it's colors, refuse to trade, and thus monopolize the entire cube!

Blockman: Any history textbook will point out clearly that the 19th century Robber Squarens operated in tandem with crooked legislators. Hardly a true Supply Side system. Besides, I'm not talking about absolute elimination of all regulations, I'm....

Jacube: Ha! Your administration has already removed the vast bulk of sensible, decent controls! What's left to protect the common square? The blockhead in the street?

Blockman: Private interest will protect him. It stands to reason that if each side wants it's own color, it'll trade to get it. A blue side with a yellow square will trade with a yellow side with a blue square. It's so simple I....

Jacube: If it's so simple, then why haven't we seen any results! Your office has been at it for over two years now!

Blockman: You'll have to remember that we inherited a terrible mess. Your party has been at it for over fifty years. I don't think it improved even one bit during that time.

Jacube: Well, we admit that in our zeal to help the common cube we perhaps overregulated some areas....

Blockman: Such as the requirement that no cube is allowed to have more than five squares of it's own color unless all the other sides have at least four of their own? There's no workable pattern that can go through that stage!

Jacube: All we were trying to do was to guarantee...

Blockman: I don't really think it is the government's place to guarantee fixed numbers of colors per side. That's the cube's own business.

Jacube: What! Have you no compassion for the common cube?

Blockman: I have plenty of compassion. But I think the best way to help the sides is to let them help themselves. We have to leave them....

Narrator: We certainly do. Join us next week for another informative debate on **Squaring Off.**

Jacube: But we worked so *hard* on those regulations! And what about all the secretaries we hired to type those rules? We employed a lot of people and now they're losing their jobs and what about.....

10
The Cubie's Anthology of Literature

Double, double toil and trouble.
Fuses burn and tempers bubble.
Cool it with a chance to solve.
Our world upon the cube revolves.
From W. Shakespeare's Macbeth.

The world of the cubie does indeed revolve upon the cube. How could it be otherwise? The cube has found a niche in every aspect of society: history, politics, religion, health and science. These subjects are the meat and potatoes of life. They represent the cold, hard facts. But the cube, that ever amazing cube, also reaches beyond the world of technical and philosophical absolutes and into the world of imagination and fantasy! It's a world that comes to life whenever a cubie puts his cube aside, reaches over and opens a book. It's the world of cubie literature!

Sadly, there are roadblocks preventing many from entering this world. The uninformed cubie, as well as a surprising number of the informed, is faced with a maddeningly disparate plethora of cubie literature and simply doesn't know where to begin reading! It is indeed a perplexing situation and has driven many a cubie (already disposed to a unique brand of McLuhanesque non-linear gestalt thought process — another roadblock) to virtual illiteracy.

In our interest to widen the intellectual horizons of all cubies, we've composed this anthology of cubie fiction. It's a sample reader that covers some of the best works from a number of different genres. Some stories will prove satisfying while others might leave you as unfulfilled as an unsolved cube. Every cubie has his or her own unique tastes. It is our hope that you at least read these selections and give them a fair chance. If we can at least interest you to look for more reading matter in one or two genres, then we will consider our mission a success. We'll have helped you break through the roadblocks and escape to the wonderful world of cubie literature! Have passport, will travel!

CUBIE FAIRY TALES

Some stories will live in the hearts of cubies for all time. The fairy tales their parents would recite to them in early cubiehood are a prime example. Who can ever forget the stories of *Goldilocks and the Three Cubes, Little Red Riding Cube,* or *Sleeping Cubie?* We certainly can't!

For those of you who led a deprived cubiehood, as well as for those of you who'd like to relive moments of the past, we've chosen to share the following classic:

Goldilocks and the Three Cubes

Once upon a time, in the land of giant forests and babbling brooks, a little girl decided to take a big walk. Her name was Goldilocks. Though she was a nice little girl, she suffered from a terrible character flaw. She was not a cubie. Why, she didn't even have a cube of her own! That explains why she was out for a walk when she should have been at home, like every good little girl and boy, working on her cube.

Goldilocks walked and walked and soon became tired of walking and was very hungry. "Oh," she exclaimed, "I do wish I had something to eat! And I also wish I had something fun to do!"

Almost as an answer to her wish, she came upon a square little house. Filled with anticipation and yearning, she rushed up to the house and knocked on the door. But there was no answer. "Dear me," uttered Goldilocks, "Whatever shall I do? There is no one home to help me!"

At length, Goldilocks decided to enter the house and help herself to whatever food and activities were available. She reasoned that if the owner was home, he or she would certainly invite her to do so.

No sooner had Goldilocks crossed the threshhold when the delicious aroma of fresh, hot porridge wafted across her senses. "Yummy!" exclaimed Goldilocks with glee. She ran into the kitchen and saw three bowls of porridge sitting on the table. She sat down at the first bowl and tried a bite. The bowl was very tiny and the porridge very hot. "Ouch!," cried Goldilocks as the porridge burnt her lip. "This is too hot for my fancy." She moved to the next chair to test the second bowl of porridge. It was a little larger than the first bowl and held just the right amount of porridge a little girl like Goldilocks should eat for one meal. It wasn't too hot, either. Still, after taking but one bite of porridge, Goldilocks couldn't help looking at the next and last bowl. She decided she'd give it a try and moved down to the next chair. It was a HUGE bowl of porridge and was actually very cold, lumpy and sticky. "Yum-yum-yummy!," shouted Goldilocks, "My favorite!" She quickly ate every last drop, and even licked the bowl clean.

"Now for some fun," mused little Goldilocks. She left the table and began to roam the house in search of an activity. It was a very bare house and it seemed as though there were no games to play. At long last she came upon three cubes. Each one had been solved. Normally, Goldilocks would never have bothered to play with a cube, but in this instance there was quite simply nothing else left to do. "Oh alright," muttered Goldilocks reluctantly, "Just this once."

The first cube was very small indeed. She fumbled and fidgeted with it for a moment or two before tossing it on the floor. "That cube is too small," said Goldilocks, though in fact, it wasn't too small. She picked up the next cube. It was larger than the first. Again, Goldilocks fumbled and fidgeted with the cube, only to finish by throwing it on the floor, "It's too medium for me," said Goldilocks, though in fact, it wasn't too medium for her at all. The third and final cube was very large. Goldilocks twisted and turned it's parts about, but soon tossed it on the floor. "It's too big for me," said Goldilocks, though in fact, it wasn't too big for her.

Leaving three terribly scrambled cubes on the floor Goldilocks decided she was tired and needed a nap. She saw three beds. The first was big and hard. The second was just the right size and softness. The third was very tiny and almost as soft as porridge. She slept in the third bed with her feet hanging over the edge.

Not too long after Goldilocks fell asleep, the three cubies who owned the house came back. The Papa cubie looked at the Mama cubie who held the Baby cubie in her arms.

"Something's not right," said the Papa cubie. The Mama cubie looked worried and the Baby cubie began to whimper. They looked in the kitchen and saw that someone had eaten all of the old, spoiled porridge that they were going to throw in the garbage. "Somebody is going to be very sick," said Mama cubie.

The cubies then looked into their bedroom and saw that a little golden haired girl had fallen asleep on the Baby cubie's bed. "It's obvious what's happened," said the Papa cubie. "This little girl has taken a walk, and satisfied her hunger and weariness here at our home. I don't mind at all. I'm glad she was taken care of." the Mama cubie mentioned something about hoping the little girl didn't get sick on the Baby cubie's bed.

Suddenly, Baby cubie began screaming and crying. The Mama and Papa cubie looked and soon began screaming and crying, too. Someone had scrambled their cubes and left them lying on the floor! Goldilocks heard the clamor and jumped up. "Have you done this to our cubes?," asked the Papa cubie. Goldilocks replied that she had.

The Mama cubie looked at her in horror. "What kind of a cubie are you?" Goldilocks replied that she wasn't any kind of a cubie at all. Upon hearing this the Papa cubie wanted to throw her out, but the Mama cubie interfered. "You poor, poor little girl! Is this true?" The Papa cubie realized the poignancy of this moment and threw his recklessness to the wind.

"Yes," answered Goldilocks, "Look at the cubes. You see, I can't solve them. I don't even know where to begin. Because of my inabilities I have spent my life trying to avoid contact with cubes and cubies. But this time, there was nothing else to do, and I was all alone, so I played with them. Oh, I know I shouldn't have! Now I feel terrible because I am reminded that I am stupid and ignorant in the ways of cubing, not to mention having scrambled someone else's cubes! Oh! boo hoo!" Goldilocks wept.

The Mama cubie and the Papa cubie didn't even need to talk about it. "Little girl, do not be sad. We can teach you some valuable tricks in cube solving. We can help you overcome your handicap."

Goldilocks stopped sniffling long enough to look up at the nice, gentle cubies. "Do you really mean that? Oh, but I couldn't! That's not fair to you!"

"Really," said the Papa cubie, "We'd like to. And after all, you've eaten our old porridge and slept on our bed. The least you can do is to accept some advice on cubing."

And Goldilocks did. In only one day she learned how to solve the cube. She went home and bought one, and to this day is having fun with it. No longer does she do silly things like take long aimless walks!

The End

SCIENCE FICTION

For the adolescent cubie, no other form of fiction has proven as popular as Science Fiction. It is also popular with many mature, educated cubies. There are many levels of science fiction — some appeals only to adolescents, some to those well versed in scientific knowledge, and others to those interested in avant garde writing, which is often very successfully used with S.F. themes. We think that the following selection will prove popular to all types of cubie science fiction readers, as well as the general public.

"I Have No Cube, And I Must Solve"

Our planet was very peaceful and beautiful. In many ways, it still is. There are green mountains capped with snows, rolling valleys and plains, mighty oceans and beautiful blue skies. We've always had these things and probably always will. For most of our history, we've enjoyed our blessings in relative peace. Oh, sure, we've had our little wars, social unrests and whatnot, but who hasn't? They come and go, just often enough to remind us how lucky we are to have a relatively peaceful and very beautiful world. But some things have changed. Our world is not the peaceful place it once was. Some fear our world will not stay beautiful. Let me tell you how this came to be.

Not too many years ago, a space ship from another planet

landed on our world. I was the Governor of the province in which they landed, so I was delegated as the official ambassador to the aliens.

The first moment I met them I feared they would be trouble for my planet. These aliens are not like you and I. One needs only to look at their faces to read their emotions and their thoughts. Why did I not heed these warnings? If only I had, you and I would today be happier, our children would be happier, and also, the aliens and their species would certainly be much happier. I should have sent them away.

But I didn't. I overlooked the greed and lust, the almost addictive need that was written across their faces when they first looked at us. Instead, I helped organize parties and parades; discussed trade agreements and cultural exchanges. As we did not yet have interplanetary space travel, the aliens were especially adamant in pursuing the possibility of building numerous spaceports over all our planet. Now I know why.

One day, after a night of salubrious partying, I was alone and talking with the captain of the space ship. He seemed a kindly man and I had taken exception to him. There was a certain sorrow in his eyes that no other officer or crew member had. He seemed reluctant about the course of life he had chosen. I asked him about it.

"Yes, I am different from the others, and I regret that I am; as it would make my task much easier."

I inquired further about this task, but he avoided answering by asking a question.

"As Governor, are you forced to make difficult decisions for the good of your citizens? To satisfy their needs? To do things you do not like to do?" I was about to reply when he continued, sadly, remotely, "I am captain of the ship, but I am not omnipotent. I cannot change the course of history. My people have a terrible need, one that is stronger than my ability to control."

Apprehensively I asked him what he was talking about. He merely shrugged his shoulders and walked quietly away from me. He stopped briefly to add what I now know was a warning: "Perhaps a long vacation, far, far away, would do you a great deal of good, my friend." Perhaps it would have, at that.

I did not have to wonder long what this terrible need of the aliens was. It happened quite suddenly the next morning. The security report that I was given told me that three of the humans, intoxicated from the previous nights party, had cornered one of my close friends, a gentle cube of old age, a genuine chip off the old block. They grabbed this poor cube and began twisting, turning and flipping him; changing every location of his squares! The poor cube's pattern, with a variety of colored squares on each of six sides, were changed! The humans had taken away his identity! What is worse, they 'finished' him. Each of his sides was a solid, uniform color when he was found. In all my years of governorship, it was the ugliest thing I had ever heard of.

I didn't have to wait long to hear of things even worse. Upon questioning the captured humans, I learned that they 'solved' — as they called it — for fun! One fellow sneered at me and revealed what I had avoided acknowledging for too long. "You stupid cube," he cackled, "you think you're so smart. You can move and communicate and think. Cubes on our planet aren't like that, but that doesn't change anything. We're going to solve you, each and every one, and don't think we can't! You're nothing but a hunk of plastic with a bunch of scrambled colored squares."

I had to leave the room and spend some time alone. "Scrambled colored squares..." indeed! Our squares are organized in a very special manner. No two cubes have the same pattern. A cube takes no greater pride than he does in his pattern. To change it is to humiliate a cube. And to change it for mere fun! The humans would have to be destroyed.

The spaceship had been successfully toppled from it's mooring and could not take off, but the remaining humans had escaped and were rampaging through small communities, solving cubes where ever they went. I saw a small town after they finished. It was pretty, in a ghastly sort of way. All the cubes had sides of the same colors. I could see where, if one regarded a cube as an inanimate object, there would be no hesitation to solve one and... but I had to stop thinking that way!

I questioned the prisoners again, one at a time in small room. After seeing the damage their peers had done, I could scarce regard them as being more than unthinking, inanimate objects.

"Why do you take such pleasure in solving us?"

"Because it's... it's fun! And it's frustrating! It's simple and it's incredibly difficult. It's — exciting when you succeed, becomes it seems far away and yet — it makes us feel good to make order out of chaos. I'd do it again if I wasn't tied up!"

"You were planning to enslave the entire planet, weren't you?"

"Yeah, but that captain, he was too slow and careful. We couldn't wait. We had to solve! There's so few cubes left on our planet and so many people — we were going to ship you talking cubes back home by the millions! And we will yet, you just wait!"

At that point, I succumbed to what had been a growing desire.

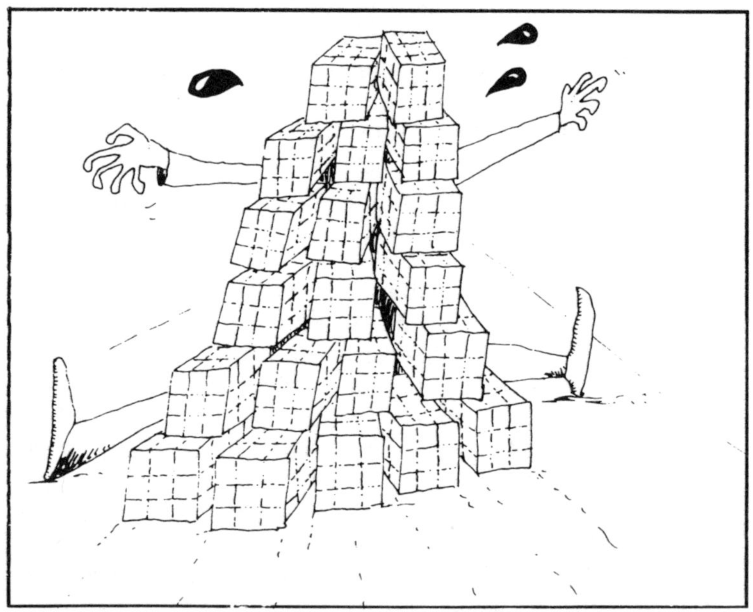

Several weeks later, I led a war party that cornered the last of the remaining humans. After the initial skirmish, I found myself chasing the captain into a dead-end ravine. He realized he was trapped and turned to face me. "I couldn't stop them! God knows I tried!"

"Don't play with me, captain, I know what you were going to do. You were going to make slaves of all of us. All my fellow cubes."

He hung his head.

"Do not feel shame," I said, for I felt sorry for the poor man.

He looked surprised.

"I understand why your fellow humans want to solve cubes. I think, if I were a cruel cube who hadn't been trained as a Governor to serve his constintuents, I would enjoy solving cubes also. I have been tempted to finish off the occasional almost solved victim your people hastily left from time to time. Sadly, I can see many of my fellow cubes are anxious to try this solving of other cubes, too. You have brought us a great and terrible knowledge, captain. Now I must see that we rebuild your spaceship, and build even more like it, and go to your world and take your people."

He looked at me with horror in his eyes.

"What are you saying?," he demanded.

"I would like to solve something, but I can claim no other cubes as my own. But I can claim you, since you are a dangerous alien."

"You mean....."

"Yes. I have no cube, and I must solve."

He didn't even scream as I began twisting his arms.

CUBEROTICA

About the time one discovers Science Fiction, one also discovers the extremely sensuous, intimate, personal relationship that can take place between cube and cubie. It is only inevitable that some cubies will attempt to describe the relationship, and the act of cubing, with the written word. We categorize this writing as 'Cuberotica'. It is intelligent, tasteful and yet still exciting and provocative. (Cuberotica is not to be confused with cubie-porn, which is a tawdry, cheap, humiliating depiction of the act of cubing). The following selection is a passage from the classic, "The Fear of Cubing".

"The Spinless Solve"

I grabbed it playfully from behind and whispered into it's upper right back corner, "Your place or mine?" I was both surprised and excited by it's answer. "Right here? But what if the guests in the other room come in and — yes, you're right, I suppose that would make it all that much better."

It didn't waste any time. It told me to shut up and not to talk. The less we knew about each other, the more mysterious, the more thrilling it would be. All I really knew about it was that it was ready for action. A few carefully directed twists and changes of colors told me that much. It went in to the bathroom and I followed. No one would miss me.

I turned the sink faucet on to let the water run and sat on the closed toilet lid. "Let's get on with it," it said.

I have never seen such a forward cube. I was beginning to feel frightened. That made it all the more exciting.

I dropped to my knees in front of it and began to touch it very aggressively. I found myself gripping it with tight, whitened knuckles and breathing heavily. It responded enthusiastically. Sensing that the surrounding called for something different, I turned it upside down. "But I've never. . ."

"Shut up!" I said, and immediately let go of it. "I'm in control now." It only whimpered for more. I began to turn it's sides and align the red side.

"Faster, faster!" it panted, and I went faster. Soon, all was a blur of color. Then, slowly and teasingly, I began to align the green squares. It moaned and squeeked so loud it hurt my ears. I hoped the running water would drown out the sound. I found myself moving faster than I wanted to, but I couldn't help it. I wanted to solve it! My back was arched, my mouth gaped open, and warm, happy sweat trickled down my face. The cube couldn't take it much longer. Neither could I. Still, I hesitated before making the final move to solve it.

"Solve me! Solve me!," it screamed. But I had had my thrills. I knew I had everything necessary to solve but the final move. I could gain no more pleasure from completing the act. But I could gain a certain titillation from standing up and walking away. Just leave that cube on the very edge of being solved, and it can't do a damn thing about it.

I stood up, readjusted my clothes and turned the water off.

"What... -I -I -," The cube looked ridiculous, almost solved, sitting there on the toilet seat, stuttering.

"You cubies are all alike!," it screamed. "All of you! I hate you! I hate you!"

I lit a cigarette and laughed enjoying the moment. "And you love every minute of it, don't you, you stupid blockhead? I'm going out to the party for another thirty minutes. I'll meet you in the back seat of my car after that and finish you off." It whimpered and I knew it'd be there.

But I wouldn't. Cubes need to be spun to be solved, but, thank God, cubies don't. We're capable of — what's that word? — the spinless solve.

I slid my cigarette under the toilet seat and flushed. The cube asked for my license number. Yes, yes, I thought, this spinless solve is going to last all night. And then some.

THE CUBE HUMOR SAMPLER

We offer an explanation instead of a selection. We've decided against including cube humor of any sort in this anthology. We feel that such humor is degrading not only to cubes, but to cubies as well. It seems to be quite the rage to make fun of various aspects of cubing, particularly in the form of cheap, tacky parodies. Although it is popular writing, we feel it has no purpose other than to humiliate — and it certainly takes no intelligence to write or to read.

Hemingway once compared writing parodies to urinating on a bathroom wall. He preferred the latter. We think the man had a point.

We urge you not to read cube humor, especially parodies. We think there are better forms of cube literature. For instance, the next selection: **Shakespeare on Cubes**, represents some of the best material ever written on the subject of cubes and cubing. And it's enjoyable.

SHAKESPEARE ON CUBES

Perhaps no other literature offers such astute comments on cubes and cubies than does that of the great, unparallelled, William Shakespeare. It is doubtful that any one man will add significantly to Shakespeare's insights. The man wrote dozens of plays and sonnets and all of them are considered classics in every aspect. Sadly, we can but offer you a few of the more famous passages from his works. If you are inspired to read more of his works, you can easily find them in any library or bookstore. Many universities offer courses in Shakespearean Cubology that you might also find beneficial.

Hamlet's Musings

To cube, or not to cube, that is the Question.
Whether 'tis nobler in the mind to suffer
The dread and anger of outrageous frustration,
Or to take action against this block of trouble,
And by confronting solve it.
To try, to fail
No more; and with success to say we end
The heart-ache and the thousand natural err's
The cube is heir to. 'tis a victory
Devoutly to be wished. To try, to solve,
To solve. Perchance to be confused.
Ay, there's the rub;
For in that paradox of confusion what scorn
may come.

Macbeth's Soliloquy

To cube, or not to cube,
Creeps in this silly place from day to day,
To the last light of evening's night.
And all our yesterdays have taunted cubies
On their way to dreary defeat. Out, out fool cube!
Life's but a walking shadow; a poor player
That twists, twirls and frets his hours upon the cube,
and then is left unsolved. It is a toy
Sold by an idiot, full of challenge and fury,
Signifying nothing.

Romeo's Plea

O solution, solution! Wherefore art thou
Solution?
Defy the cube and refuse it's pride,
Or, if thou wilt not, be but sworn to counsel,
Or I'll no longer be a cubie.
'Tis but the squares that are my enemy,
Thou are thyself just within grasp.
What's solving? 'tis not all orange, nor red,
Nor blue, nor green, nor any other part

Without the whole match. O, be some other color!
What's is a solution? That which we call a cube,
By any other name would cause equal rage
In thou were it not for your
Elusive perfection which is owned.
Yield fond help and doff thy mystery;
And for that answer, which is no part of me,
Solve all my cube.

EXISTENTIAL CUBISM

Are you a cubie who's into heaviosity? If so, the literature of existentialism could be for you. Though the literature of this philosophical movement is not the most entertaining or thrilling literature available, it can present a challenge to the mind that is almost as satisfying to comprehend as a cube is to solve. Many readers will read and reread stories and novels of existential cubism trying to decipher their meanings. Some succeed, some fail. But in the world of existential cubism, does it really matter if one understands? Or is it important that one merely asks the question? If you are intrigued by the puzzles of existential cubism, inquire at a university library for more reading material. Our selection is a very, very short abridgement of Franz Kafka's three thousand page novel: *Looking Through a Glass Cube.*

Looking Through a Glass Cube

I sit here in the late night, staring at my cube. I notice the oil in my lamp is running low and remind myself to fill it in the morning. Such trivialities. And I wonder: Does the cube know of such trivialities? Does it care if the lamp is low in oil?

In my chair, locked into this fat, obese body that smells like sweating pork flesh, I continue to look at the cube. If squares could talk. I look at the cube and try to peer inside. Does it have a soul? A mind? Does it think? Is it repulsed by my appearance as much as I am? Does it shudder when I touch it?

Bah! The ramblings of a fat, misunderstood poet in the late night as seen by the light of a dim lamp.... I am a fool. Still, I look into the cube. Certainly it is looking into me. Does it understand the cruelties of life better than I? Can it appreciate pain and sorrow and suffering, or is that the realm of mortal flesh alone?

$$-\text{o}-$$

The morning light shines into my eyes. I must have fallen asleep in the chair. It is so hard to move when one is a giant of flesh and the night is dark....But wait!

Tell me I am dreaming! Tell me this is a cruel hoax my mind is forging upon itself! *I am outside of my body looking at myself!* Is this the release promised by death? To waste eternity staring at the fetid corpse? But no, the body moves, it breathes.....

Now I understand. I am inside the cube. I am trapped within that box of mystery, that idiot savant, that child's game and philosopher's touchstone. The cube.

It is strange. I am a victim of an experience beyond the range of human understanding, and yet there are no bombshells, no trumpets blaring, no ceremonies, no gossip behind the scenes. It — my exchange — has been done simply and quietly. I am inside the cube, for better or worse. And — what is inside my old body? (*'old body'* — already I have accepted the whims of destiny.)

It's eyes open wide. The face gesticulates. The teeth are coated with phlegm and mucous. Still, the face smiles at me. The body stands and roars with laughter. And suddenly, knowledge fills me like light filling the darkness. Trapped within my old body is the spirit of this cube in which I am now encased. It is so obvious that a young child could understand it. It happened after I fell asleep, after perusing the possibility of the cube existing as a spiritual entity, after I wondered if squares could talk, what stories they would tell.

Yes! Yes! It is a grand glorious joke, and I laugh silently along with my old, despicable body and the spirit of the cube. For certainly it wondered the same of me. We have each been granted our wish, as easily as a magick genie would grant it's master! We have become the answer to our own questions.

I stop laughing abruptly. Life is a cruel prankster, I remind myself. Why should life be kind and obliging to anyone, let alone a poet who scratches his dribbling lines in a tattered notebook?

How long has it been since that day? A week? A year? I have lost all track of time. I seem to have even lost all comprehension or concern for time.

My old body, laughing and roaring, walked out of the house that day. I should have understood sooner why it had not stopped laughing when I had. On the way out the door, it shouted to my mother upstairs "Tell Nataya that I am bound for the Caspian to embark on a career as a sailor!" The Caspian? A sailor? I did not understand him, and I knew for all certainty that my poor, darling Nataya would never understand.

—o—

After sitting for days, Nataya picks me up and sits in the same chair I had once sat in. She seems happy, happier than I have ever known her. I do not allow myself to consider the justification of this joy. After all, all joy is shallow. Only sorrow is capable of depth, and even then only on rare occasions.

She spins my sides about and makes feeble attempts to solve the mystery of combining equal colors on all sides. Still, the efforts are genuine and bring her happiness. Suddenly, I am incredulous at my own feelings. I am excited, I am on the verge of a great discovery, a verge that I have seen prior only from a distance while immersed in great, genuine pain and suffering.... I am on the verge.... The verge of total understanding! Oh, Natya, do not stop, I beg of you!

All the mysteries of life are taking shape: From whence do we come and for what purpose do we proceed? Why have we not been told the answers? Why does the sound of wind blowing through the leafless trees of late autumn bring water to my eyes? Why must the greater workings of the mind be crouched in pain? These mysteries were becoming clear. I can see an answer looming in the distance, and with each move of my cube that the innocent Nataya executes, the answer looms ever closer. The wisdom of the ancients is within arms length! Oh! Only in my most deranged flights of fancifulization had I considered the possibility of becoming one with such knowledge! It is too much for me — but no, it isn't too much. I had thought my psyche could not contain omniscience, but I was wrong (ah, but what could a feeble poet comprehend, eh?). Now I am a cube. Life itself is within my grasp.

Ah, Nataya, your sleek hands the color of fresh goat's milk are giving me more pleasure than they ever gave me in our bed! Already I know that it does not matter how fast you turn my sides and align the colored squares, for all knowledge is timeless.

If I could, talk to you, my Nataya, my little bleating lamb, I would tell you the immensity of my love — not the love of my old self, but the love of my new spirit, the one bathed in knowledge. If I could but share this....

But wait! The door opens and Nataya sets me back on the table, nearly solved, but still, very unsolved. She rushes to meet a tall, dark, handsome man in the uniform of the Commisar! He takes her in his arms and she swoons beneath the relentless pressure of his lips and his hands......

I am crestfallen.

But there is more. On the divan, across from the very chair I once sat in, this mindless servant of the state takes my Nataya and has his way with her. I have been cheated! My old body leaves for some reckless adventurism in the Caspian Sea, and my Nataya, my always faithful Nataya, my one pillar of strength against all sorrow and pain.....

And more. She has her way with him. Her wildly gyrating body does more things than I had thought possible — certainly, considering the dimensions of my old body, some of the things were physically impossible, but nonetheless.... She had never perspired while making love with me, I'll have you know!

Later, her lover picks me up and laughs. With four moves he solves me and tosses me aside to again take Nataya. Four moves! I am filled with all the answers to all questions. *I am the knowledge of the universe!* Yet, I am not thrilled. I am saddened. For of what use is all knowledge when the one I love is riding atop another man? I have seen eternity and heaven and they have slapped me in my face and reminded me that I am forever unworthy of such knowledge.

My optimism and proud bearing shall be punished. I can see that it must be. I shall live forever in this cube, a plaything of the idle hands of idle minds.

The oil in the lamp runs out and darkness descends. I recall that I did not fill it on the eve of my exchange. It is better that I did not, for now I cannot see the antics my Nataya is engaged in. I can only hear her laugh and scream.

And I am reminded of the laugh given by my old body as it left the house that first morning. He was happy, finally, to have changed places with a wretched poet and to no longer see life looking through a glass cube.

CUBE MYSTERIES

One of the most popular forms of cube literature that appeals to all audiences is that of the cube mystery. Whether you're young or old, male or female, smart or stupid, you're bound to enjoy a good "whodunit". Our selection is none other than a story featuring the famous, legendary Sherlock Holmes! The most masterful mystery matriculator of them all! This story, as recounted by the good Doctor Watson, is one of the best. Even if you've read it a dozen times, you'll enjoy reading it again.

The Case of the Cubie's Final Solution

Many is the time I've seen the great Sherlock Holmes solve a difficult case, but never was I so impressed with his powers of analytical observation and deductive thinking than when I saw them employed in the case that has come to be known as "The Cubie's Final Solution".

It all started one evening while I was paying a social visit to Holme's residence at 221B Baker Street. As usual, Holmes proved a very entertaining host. He displayed his uncanny prowess with the cube, creating unique patterns of colors with disarming rapidity.

"Good gracious, man, how do you do that?" I never ceased to be awed with his cubing skills.

"Elementary, my dear Watson. Any child who can add the numbers one plus one and arrive at two can do these things with a cube." I fear I had quite broken the magic of the moment, for he summarily tossed the cube into a pile of bric-a-brac he had collected from some number of previous cases.

"I say, Holmes, isn't that —" I never finished my question, for there sounded on the door a loud, rapid knocking. Holmes smiled. "Come in, Tommy," he said. I never had a chance to ask Holmes how he knew it was Tommy, for the young neighborhood boy burst in and spewed forth the most amazing bit of news.

"Mr. Holmes, sir, pardon me, and hullo to you, too, Doctor Watson, there's been something terrible happened at the

Crown Hall down the road, sir, and I thought I...." The lad had to stop for air, he was so excited.

"Easy there, Tommy," said Holmes, leaning back in his high-backed chair and lighting his pipe, "Nothing could be so important as to cause you to die of strangulation."

"No sir, maybe not, sir, but all's the same — *England's Champion Cubie's done been murdered!* Not by five minutes, I swear!"

Holmes jumped to his feet, gathered his cape and coat, and then stopped to look at me. "Well, are you coming along or aren't you?" he demanded?

"But -wh -where are you going?" I managed to blubber.

"Confound, man, to solve the case!" Of course I'd follow! I leaped up and followed him forthwith.

—o—

Reginald Aldridge, the reigning cubie champion of England for six years running, had been stabbed in the cubic chest while in his dressing room at the Crown Hall. He had been preparing for a charity cubing contest against a new cubie hotshot from Liverpool. Holmes and I looked down at his body. His cube was still in his hand. I was quite touched. I knew Holmes was, too, but he was acting as a professional and couldn't reveal his emotions at this most critical time.

Inspector Winklebottoms, Scotland Yard, was just finishing taking some notes on his final interview. "Thank you, Mrs. Aldridge, you get some rest now."

Holmes interjected with presumed authority — an authority that comes from confidence, not arrogance. "Do you mind if I ask a few questions, Inspector Winklebottoms?"

"Oh....I should have figured you'd be here before too long." "Ask 'em now as soon as later, I suppose. Though I'll have all you need in the official report."

Holmes merely smiled. Winklebottoms snorted.

"This here's Saunders Walcott, Aldridge's trainer and manager."

Holmes shook his hand. "Our country has lost a great cubie, Mr. Walcott. We owe it cubies the world over to find the murderer."

"Anything I can do to help, Mr. Holmes, I will." The old fellow — bald and with quite an unhealthy paunch — seemed genuinely shaken by the incident. Holmes began the questioning.

"You must have been quite close to Aldridge. You've been his manager for nigh on ten years, I believe." The man nodded. "Tell me, was Aldridge a gambling man? Did he have any debts needed paying off — any he was late in paying off?

The man was justly insulted. I was, myself, amazed at Holme's impetuosity. I couldn't help but reprimand him. "See here, Holmes," I ventured, "That's no way to talk to the manager of the highly respected Aldridge!" Holmes gave me but one warning look. I checked myself and sealed my lips. I believe I mumbled something about seeing to the health of the widow. Fortunately, I managed to overhear the rest of the questioning.

Walcott replied that Aldridge had no connection with any figure of the underworld. He stayed away from it, though the temptation was high for one with his money and fame. "After all," said Walcott, "He wouldn't be doing a charity cubing contest if he was in need of money, now, would he?"

"I don't know," said Holmes, "Would he?"

"I - well, he might at that. Always did too many of them from my point of view, anyway, for what that's worth."

Holmes studied the face of Walcott more carefully. He then turned to a nattily attired young man who looked to have no problem with the women.

"You're Jimmy Cooke. The supposed brash young cubie from Liverpool. I've seen your picture in the Time. This was to have been your first match with Aldridge, am I not correct?"

"Yes, I'm sorry the chap died. Now they'll never know I was capable of beating the champion."

Inspector Winklebottoms jumped in. "See here, lad, that's just the kind of thing that makes you our number one suspect! Holmes, we've got a report that he had a private cubing match with Aldridge earlier in the day and was soundly beaten. They had quite an argument after that. There's justification to believe he killed Aldridge to avoid being embarrassed at this evening's match!"

Holmes paid no heed to Winklebottom's theory. It seemed to make perfect sense to me. Instead, Holmes pulled a terribly scrambled cube from his pocket. "What say we race, young Jimmy?"

Jimmy laughed and shook his head. Winklebottoms demanded to know how Holmes could insult this grevious occasion.

"Pay attention, and you'll learn, Inspector Winklebottoms. Let me put it this way, Jimmy. If you compete with me I think I can get you off the hook."

Jimmy's eyes brightened. "But I haven't my cube."

Walcott darted for the cube in Aldridge's blood smeared hands. "Here, use..."

Holmes moved faster than a cold wind and grabbed Walcott's wrist. "Don't touch that cube!" He glared at everyone in the room. "Don't anyone touch it!" At that point someone offered a scrambled cube to Jimmy Cooke.

"Are you sure you want to do this, Mr. Holmes?" I don't want to ruin your reputation. I'm fast. Faster than Aldridge ever was."

"We'll soon see. Go!" They commenced to solve their cubes with great speed and dexterity. I admit I've never seen anyone move as fast as Jimmy. I must also admit that Holmes was not moving as fast as he could have. Was he playing with young Jimmy? What mysterious, ingenious plan was Holmes executing?

Jimmy finished before Holmes. It wasn't a record by any means, but under the circumstances that would have been expecting too much of the man.

"Amazing," said Holmes, "Yet I really don't know what I could have done to go any faster."

Jimmy glanced at Holmes' cube. "There are quite a few things you could have done. If I may?" Holmes handed the cube to Jimmy. Jimmy showed him. I didn't understand what they were talking about. I know something of cubing, but not on the high level that Holmes and Jimmy Cooke operate on.

"Brilliant, brilliant," said Holmes. "You've made quite an impression on me, young man."

Inspector Winklebottoms pointed to the poor woman who sat beside me, Mrs. Aldridge. "That's the widow, Holmes. I don't mean to sound cruel, but she's on my list, too."

"Of course you don't mean to sound cruel, Inspector. You're simply doing your job." Only my long years of close association with Holmes enabled me to detect the subtle, condescending sarcasm in his voice. "And what — and forgive me for my stupidity — is the motive?"

Winklebottoms assumed an air of smugness. "The motive? Well now, Holmes, it'd be obvious to any seasoned Scotland Yard detective. It's the money."

"Hello! You don't mean to say —" Holmes was toying with him.

It's very possible. She may have killed him for his money. It's obvious he stayed close to the coin. Look at her clothing — baggy, drab, second hand. She wanted to have some fun with the money, and the only way she could get at it...." Winklebottoms gestured to the dead Aldridge.

I dare say the poor woman burst into tears. "Come now, Winklebottoms," I replied angrily — after all, the woman was more or less under my care at the moment - "That's no way to treat the bereaved. If you're wrong - and I think you are - I demand that you apologize to this dear woman on your knees!"

"There, there Watson," said Holmes. "This is always an awkward moment for the close survivors. But you are correct in that Mrs. Aldridge is innocent?"

"Yes. Mrs. Aldridge, may I be so bold as to announce that you are — due to have a child in six and one half months?"

Mrs. Aldridge looked up with the slightest trace of a smile. "That's right. Exactly six and a half months to the day."

"How did you know that, Holmes?," I asked.

"Watson, from observing the size of her midsection!"
Winklebottoms protested that this did not make her innocent.

"But it does destroy your case, Inspector. The poor woman
didn't need money to buy clothes. I'm sure she has a large
wardrobe of fine clothing. But due to her temporary size, she
needs larger clothes. So she borrowed some — she impresses
me as not an extravagant spender — probably from her
mother, for the duration of her pregnancy." Mrs. Aldridge said
he was correct. Winklebottoms began to mutter when Holmes
continued.

"Aldridge was a good, clean, charitable man. I don't think
a good cubie like he would have married a woman any less his
equal. Certainly she'd be more concerned with properly raising her child than with having free reign of her husband's earnings. I don't think she'd kill the father of her child."

Winklebottoms frowned. "Well, like I said, this Jimmy
Cooke here is still the number one suspect."

"I don't see why," offered Holmes.

Winklebottoms stomped his foot and raised his voice.
"Because he wanted to eliminate his biggest competitor,
the only man who could solve a cube faster than he!"

"Hardly. I think he could have beaten Aldridge tonight.
And Jimmy thinks so too. Why bother killing him?"

"You think he could have beaten him, but I don't, and I'm
the official inspector. What about their match this afternoon?"

Holmes smiled and looked at Jimmy. "Jimmy is a smart
competitor. He knew he'd be nervous the first time he challenged the champion, so he did it in an unofficial, private
meeting. Got the bugs out of his system, so to speak. Earlier,
Jimmy showed me some pointers on cubing that show me he's
an absolute cubing genious. I'm familiar with Aldridge's
techniques, and they wouldn't have beaten Jimmy's. The loss
this afternoon? Blame it on the jitters. A nervous hand that
slipped once or twice." I looked at Jimmy and saw that this
was true. He said nothing, being too proud to admit to why he
was defeated.

"Then why was they arguin'?" Winklebottoms was too impatient. I knew Holmes would get to the bottom of things soon
enough. He was in no hurry. After all, Holmes was now in his
glory. He pulled his pipe out and lit it while talking.

"The argument? I can't say for sure, but it probably concerned Aldridges retirement."

Jimmy, Mrs. Aldridge and Mr. Walcott all dropped their mouths! Winklebottoms laughed. "Now why would a champion in his prime go be retirin'?"

"But it's true," said Mrs. Aldridge.

"I'd say in another six months," continued Holmes, "Just prior to the birth of the child. Aldridge had the money to live comfortably for the rest of his life. He wanted to be the perfect father and spend plenty of time with his child - impossible for a champion cubie. So he planned to retire — one month before the championships where Jimmy would have handily beaten him. Nothing infuriates a challenger more than having the champion hand him the crown on a platter without a chance to prove himself worthy of it."

"I'll question the witnesses on the matter of the topic of the argument, Holmes." Winklebottoms sighed. He hated having to ask his next question and delayed it as long as possible. But all eyes were upon him. He succumbed to the pressure. "Then, who did kill Aldridge?"

"I'm afraid our dear Saunders Walcott is your man, Inspector."

Walcott jumped and two bobbies grabbed him and held him firm. "You can't prove anything, *Sherlock Holmes*! It's all a guess on your part! All guessing!"

Holmes puffed rapidly on his pipe. "You don't make for much of a challenge, Walcott. You earn ten percent of all Aldridge's earnings. When he retires - was to have retired - you'd earn nothing. And Aldridge had a propensity for charities — and again your earnings are nothing. You commented earlier, with a noticeable degree of disdain for a companion and partner of ten years, that Aldridge gave too many charity performances of his cubing skills. That set me to thinking."

Holmes paused and exhaled a cloud of smoke.

"By the way, from the look of the wound, I'd say you used a scabbard made by the Jahnrabe tribe of northeast India that you purchased during Aldridge's world tour of three years ago. Am I right? Well, the inspector's men will find it soon enough. You can't have hidden it too far away." Walcott fairly bristled with rage.

"You gave me the deciding clue, Walcott, when you reached for Aldridge's cube. Besides the embarrassingly gauche act of using a dead champion's cube in a contest - which would have given you a gruesome satisfaction - you realized, too late, that Aldridge might have left a clue in his arrangement of the cube."

Holmes picked the cube up and tossed it to Jimmy.

"Don't change anything, Jimmy, just examine it closely. If I'm not mistaken, it's arranged so that there are two different ways to solve it in ten moves, no more, no less."

After a moment, Jimmy replied, "You're quite right, Mr. Holmes. It's a unique arrangement."

"I should say so, Jimmy. Forty-three quintillion to one are the odds that it would be arranged like that by accident. It's actually far more difficult to put the cube in that position than it is to solve it."

Winklebottoms scratched his head.

"Precisely," said Holmes. "Walcott left him before he was dead, giving Aldridge the chance to leave us the clue. A clever man."

"But what's the clue?" asked Winklebottoms. He wasn't terribly bright. Even I saw the clue.

"Elementary, Winklebottoms. Two tens. Only Walcott's association with Aldridge carries two tens. Ten percent of the earnings, and ten years in partnership."

"Coincidence!" shouted Walcott. He found no sympathy. He hung his head and finally gave up. "Very well. I did it. I hated him for wanting to retire and wanting to do all these profitless charities. *I made him what he was!* He owed something to me, didn't he? He couldn't just quit and leave me to starve? That's not right, is it?

"Take him away," said Winklebottoms to the bobbies.

"That was quite a display of reasoning, Holmes," I said to him back in his home.

Holmes puffed his pipe silently in the dim lights.

"I say, Holmes, I knew you were up to something when you muddled your way through that cubing contest. I knew you could go faster."

"I wanted to give young Jimmy a chance to feel superior. A proud man will boast and share his intelligence, reflecting his true skills, which in his case, are great indeed."

"Well, good thing you didn't embarrass the chap. He'd have given up professional cubing for sure."

Holmes seemed surprised by my observation. "How do you come to know so much about professional cubies, Watson?"

"I treat a number of common ailments — cramped fingers, strained eyesight. That sort of thing."

"Nothing serious?" he asked.

"No."

"That's good. Very good." He smiled and turned away from me. I don't know if he meant it was good that cubies didn't suffer from anything worse, or good that I didn't treat them for worse.

I shall always remember the case of "The Cubie's Final Solution". Fortunately, I had the chance to share many other great adventures with Holmes before he retired to Sussex to solve cubes. Perhaps one day I can share another adventure with you.

11
Astrology Guide for Cubing

Having trouble solving the cube and can't figure out why? You think it's merely a matter of physics and statistical planning? Hardly. It takes more than formulas or meditation to solve the cube. It takes a *solver*. You. And you bring more with you than your memory of patterns and plans. You bring with you your own character, your persona, your unique identity. The latter have far more to do with solving the cube than you would think. It stands to reason, then, that the more you know yourself, the more control you can exercise over the cube. In our desire to help you in solving the cube, we've compiled a reliable and accurate Astrological Guide and related it directly to cube solving. You think astrology is a bunch of mumbo jumbo? Don't laugh. You haven't solved the cube yet, have you? You need every scrap of help you can get, and knowing the traits of your sun-sign can't hurt.

ARIES (March 21 - April 20)

You are fiery, impulsive, and as an Aries you will dash headfirst into cube solving, naively thinking a simple solution will be forthcoming merely because you want it so. Your selfish side will probably be thwarted and you will soon lose interest if your desired solution is not met immediately. You will never again think about the Cube.

TAURUS (April 21 - May 21)

As all folks born with this sign, you are placid and sensible. A Taurus may have the best chance of all other signs when it comes to solving the cube, and being one you will stubbornly stick to the task at hand and abandon all other life commitments until you solve it. This relentless application will probably bring you most success in solving the cube, but you will remain lonely all of your life.

GEMINI (May 22 - June 21)

The dual sign of Gemini gives you twice the advantage of all other signs, especially if you can stop your restless fidgeting long enough to give cubing a try. You are versatile, clever and will certainly find a solution somewhere in your reserve of talents, but your inherent impatience, along with not learning by your own mistakes and blaming strangers for your misfortune are your greatest stumbling blocks.

CANCER (June 22 - July 22)

You tenacious crab. Good luck with cubing, 'cause everyone knows that you think yourself above cubing. Yet, you may succeed if you could ever decide which approach to take. As with most crabs, the direct approach is out of the question. Cancer's patience is a plus for all problem solving, but your susceptibility to howling at the moon may change your moods to be frivolous and you forget where you leave the cube. Your retention abilities are far too limited. Take up rolling beach balls.

LEO (July 23 - August 23)

Your high strung, energetic nature may be the reason behind all Leo's first attempts at solving the cube. Your tyranical pride will be the reason for not putting it down until it's solved. All Leos need to dominate, to feel superior, and you will not let defeat get the better of you, although you will never solve the cube. Cheating is your only salvation.

VIRGO (August 24 - September 23)

Poor, poor Virgo. A puzzle such as the cube is like a thorn in your side. Your methodical pickiness will have a field day with cubing and your natural tendency to be a worrier will not let you quit until you find a working solution. Virgo's need for exactness will not rest with a cube out of order. You simply must put things right.

LIBRA (September 24 - October 23)

The alert, intelligent Libra is compelled to seek balance in all things, even cubing. You will carefully weigh all the possibilities, analyze all the possibilities and then painstakingly find the inevitable balance of colors that your cube requires. No one will understand your solution.

SCORPIO (October 24 - November 22)

The determined Scorpio *will* find a solution to the cube, or we shall all beware of your wrath! If you should fail, you must have revenge. The seemingly cool and removed Scorpio is a most forceful competitor. If the cube could be solved by sheer willfulness alone, Scorpio would be the victor.

SAGITTARIUS (November 23 - December 21)

As a Sagittarius you may be insatiably curious but your impatience with the petty details of cubing will soon get the better of you. Sagittarius, known for candid frankness, may be the only one of us all to actually ask what all the fussing with this silly cube is about.

CAPRICORN (December 22 - January 20)

Capricorn, another persevering character, may have good fortune with the cube. Fortunately, your steady discipline is founded on a noble ambition, not just plain, plodding stubborness. A Capricorn's reserved, hard-working nature will solve the cube for reward, not simply to be solving a puzzle. It might be worthy to mention that Saturn's influence over Capricorn could prove detrimental. (The force of the rings over the squares).

AQUARIUS (January 21 - February 19)

The probing Aquarius must try to find an answer to the cube. It is your nature to investigate the mysterious. You may be broad-minded enough to try anything, but you are also rebellious enough to fling tradition aside and simply give up the task if you feel like it. After all, as an Aquarius you are famous for your incapacity to settle down to anything for very long.

PISCES (February 20 - March 20)
Pisces has a meditative, imaginative nature, but your head is often in the
clouds, and that is not a good vantage point for cubing. As the dreaming,
impractical Pisces, you may spend more time contemplating the future of cubing rather than actually cubing itself. But beware! The sensitive Pisces may
become overly melancholy about your inabilities to solve the cube. You should
remember that you are not particularly suited to any competition and stress.

12
Zen and the Art of Cubing

experience the challenge of cubing
welcome the frustration of cubing
for it will help you grow
with time the act of cubing will become as natural
as breathing
and the goal of six matched sides
becomes secondary to the meditative joy of cubing

begin your cubing in a square room
if you like, for inspiration
any solitary cubicle will do

find a point of focus on your cube
meditate on the process and outcome of your
efforts

let the colors wander through your mind
you might begin with blue
as the calm and soothing sky
or white
the essence of purity
for a fiery beginning, red or orange
or yellow, color of the life giving sun
maybe you will choose green
to remind you of mother earth's
springtime

wherever you choose to begin
it is your choice
no one else can decide for you

you may lose interest
you may feel incapable
but square your shoulders to the task
let the twirling and flipping of the
squares sweep you along
let the flow of color and movement
carry you
and you will see beautiful patterns form

a sense of timelessness will come over you
your fingers will seem to move
the colored squares effortlessly
the motion may become your sole
sense of purpose
and the destination or act of
finishing will lose importance
next to the experience of the moment

don't force yourself to get the yellow
side finished first
or the red or any other color
you mustn't feel boxed in
be patient and you will be rewarded
as the squares seem to slip
into place by magic

it is not necessary to compete with the
eight year old neighborhood boy who can do
the cube in thirty seven point oh nine five two seconds
you have your own unique pace
this is your time to play and experience
the joy of doing it your way

no one, no book can tell you
where to start
what moves to make
what is right
how to twirl or flip
only you can discover what is right
for you
is doing so, you will expand
life will seem fuller and richer
and if you reach the goal
if you finish the task
begin the meditative cycle again

for your joy is not in the accomplishment
of this singular task
not the completion of the actual
physical act
your sense of victory is the process
through which you have traveled
in the moments spent reaching the end

not the arrival of the end
your purpose has not been simply to do the cube
but to use the cubing as a consciousness
raising
and thereby
make yourself a more well rounded
human being

you'll be happy with this approach to cubing
for the odds are so tremendously against
your ever completing the cube
you'll need a rationalization
to explain your actions

13
An Open Letter
From the Inhumane Society

Dear Zen of Cubing Reader,

The Inhumane Society is a not-for-only-profit group formed to prevent cruelty to inhuman objects. In the past, we have written and lobbied for proposed legislative bills, sponsored lectures and workshops, developed a student education program, and created halfway houses — all to help prevent and alleviate cruel treatment to a variety of objects — including shoes, automobiles, and record albums. Though we have had considerable success, our job is never finished.

We've recently been made aware of a horrid new form of inanimate abuse. Cube Abuse. Why people would want to inflict damage on cubes is beyond our comprehension. Cubes are simple, multi-colored little puzzles. They hurt no one. Yet people hurt them.

Why? Mostly because people are frustrated at their own inability to solve the puzzle of the cube. They vent their feelings on the innocent, inanimate object. In an effort to avoid confrontation with the source of their frustration, people will hide cubes in dark drawers and closets, stuff them into bags, and even throw them in the garbage! This is no way to treat a cube! A cube likes to exist in clean, well lit open areas where its colors can shine and catch the attention of people.

An even worse form of abuse is outright torture. Some incompetent cube solvers have been known to smash a cube to bits with hammers or other large objects. Others have used irritating toxic paints to 'touch up' the sides to make the cube appear to have been properly solved. This is not the worst of the abuses, but for reasons of common decency we shall not describe the uglier forms.

Possibly the most common form of abuse is to ignore a cube after a few futile attempts at solving it. For weeks, even months, a cube may sit lonely on a shelf, unspun, untwirled, even unflipped. The despair and uselessness that a cube feels is unimaginable.

All that any cube asks for from humans is an open place to reside, simple maintenence, and occasional but regular use. If this is too much for you to provide, then perhaps you shouldn't own a cube.

Obviously, if there were less cubes, there would be less abuse. Cubes would fall into the hands of people who truly wanted them. Unfortunately, with the proliferation of 'cubie farms', the population of cubes seems unlikely to drop. (You might consider having your cube mitered.).

If you wish to help end the national shame of cube abuse, please send us a donation. Even a dollar will help. The Inhumane Society is working day and night to prevent cruelty to cubes and all other inhuman objects. Thank you for your concern.

Thank you,

Leslie Abigale Spinner
Co-ordinator, The Inhumane Society

14
The Kama Sutra of Cubing

BY
Khubba La Shantiyama

Only with the full understanding of all aspects of a subject can one maximize his or her pleasure with that subject. It is with this reasoning that we sought to write of, in a public form, the joys of intimate cubing. This is a subject which has heretofore been limited to locker room and bathroom discussion. By the callous and uneducated, intimate cubing has been discussed only in the most vulgar terms. When attempts are made by concerned people to discuss it with some intelligence, it's always done with whispers and a great sense of inhibitive embarrassment. We feel it's time for a significant change in attitude.

Kama Sutra of Cubing offers you, for the first time, intelligent, straightforward, unabashed advice on how to achieve the maximum pleasure from your most intimate cubing experiences. Some of our suggestions will excite you and fill your cubing experiences with a greater sensual pleasure than you've ever imagined possible. Other suggestions, for some people, will bring laughter and ridicule. Others may make you gag.

Our advice is not to be taken blindly. You must determine for yourself the areas you wish to explore. We hope, though, that you are mature enough not to let old puritan standards inhibit your pleasure. If some particular practice seems enticing to you, try it with honest enthusiasm. Don't avoid it simply because it doesn't seem 'right', or, "my mother would never do such a thing".

NICK-NICK and YA-YA
(Relationships)

To begin discussion of the myriad ways of increasing your cubing pleasure, it is first necessary to discuss the "nick" and "ya-ya" (relationship), with your cube:

NICK-NICK
(Importance of Respect)

You and your cube must have a certain sense of respect for each other, especially you for the cube. It's an old maxim that your sense of self worth is measured by the way you treat the one you solve. Think about it. Do you hold your cube in low esteem? Keep it locked in a drawer for days on end? Leave it lying around where the dog can abuse it? If you treat your cube with such disdain, how can you ever hope to achieve more than a base, animalistic pleasure from cubing?

Our research has shown that the happiest cubing experiences are had by people who have an honest, caring relationship with their cube, along, of course, with a proper sense of respect. If you aren't already one of these people, now's the time to change.

YA-YA
(Expectation)

Remember that your cube has it's own unique identity. Don't coerce it to partake in practices that it has no desire for. Cubing is a shared, two-way experience and cannot be dictated by one person. Don't create expectations that your cube can't live up to. It's not only unfair to the cube, it's unfair to you. You should enjoy your relationship for what it is: The voluntary sharing of mutual ground by two unique entities.

VULVA CUBIS
(Things Change)

As your relationship with your cube continues through the years, remember that there are going to be changes. Nothing remains constant. Don't be dissappointed by these changes, whatever they may be. If your relationship is based on respect and concern, you'll find the strength to cope with these changes, and perhaps to even find that they strengthen your relationship. Welcome change with open hands.

KAMA CUBIS
(Cubing Techniques)

There are as many ways to cube as there are people and cubes. There is no one 'correct' method. The only correct method is the one, or ones, that you and your cube decide are right for you. There is a 'most common' method, however, which is employed by most uneducated, unliberated, bungling partners. These people would have you believe that their way of cubing is the 'right way'. Don't fall for it. What you do with your private life is your business.

On the other hand, it's our business to *offer advice* on the various aspects of intimate cubing. We hope that you find the discussion of the following topics interesting and beneficial.

LOCUS CUBUS
(Where to Cube)

The traditional cubing ground is in a quiet, secluded room of your home; a bedroom, a study, even the living room couch. The reasons are obvious. The privacy and quietness allow you to free your attention and focus it on cubing and cubing alone. You don't need to worry about being interrupted. We agree that for most people, most of the time, these places are the best and most practical in which to cube.

But for some people, some of the time, it gets boring to cube in the same old place all of the time. A change of locale can work wonders and rejuvinate all aspects of your cubing life. Try some other rooms — the basement workbench, the bathtub, or on top of a running vacuum cleamer — you'll be amazed!

Beyond your front door, the whole world awaits you. Some people find it particularly thrilling to cube in public places where they might be discovered. We've had people tell us about out-of-this-world experiences they've had cubing in elevators, stairwells, public restrooms, back seats of buses and parks.

If your are interested in cubing beyond your front door but have never before attempted it, plan carefully for the first adventure. The last thing you want is to have a problematic, traumatic first experience. Although, you may find it even more exciting to be watched by total strangers while cubing.

TEMPO CUBA
(Frequency)

You can cube as often or as seldom as you wish. Some people are satisfied with cubing once or twice a month, others find they are restless unless they do it at least once a day. There's certainly no reason why you can't do it several times per day — or session. No known physical damage has been known to occur to those who cube frequently (otherwise known as cubomaniacs).

CUBA-CUBA and FLIP-FLOP
(Foreplay, Duration and Afterplay)

The act of cubing is in many ways like a good story. It has a beginning, middle and end. Careful attention is needed for each aspect to help create a fulfilling experience.

Foreplay (Cuba) is very important. It provides a transition from the bothersome daily worries of life to the beautiful, other-worldliness of cubing, where the mind must be free of all matters but the one in hand. Rarely does one jump directly into the act of cubing.

Your foreplay can be gentle and soothing, or it can be aggressive and tension releasing. It can take as short a time as a few seconds, or it can take an entire evening. Some people intentionally prolong their foreplay to build the atmosphere to highly charged levels.

The duration (Cuba-Cuba) of the act of cubing is also a matter of personal choice, though on an average, it usually lasts around forty-five minutes. It's difficult to maintain a sufficient level of intensity and interest for much longer than this (for most people). This is not to say that cubing must be conducted at a fevered pitch at all times. You can cube very peacefully, even distractedly, and still have a satisfying experience. Even then, the act rarely goes beyond the average forty-five minutes.

Afterplay (Flip-Flop) is an oft neglected part of cubing. Once the solution has occurred, many people feel the act of cubing is over. This is not so. One does not climb to the top of a mountain and jump off, one walks back down.

Admire your accomplishment. Look at all sides of the cube. The tension is gone now, relax and enjoy. Spin some of the squares around to create fun patterns. Laugh. Meditate on how fulfilling this act of cubing has been and what it means in your relationship with the cube.

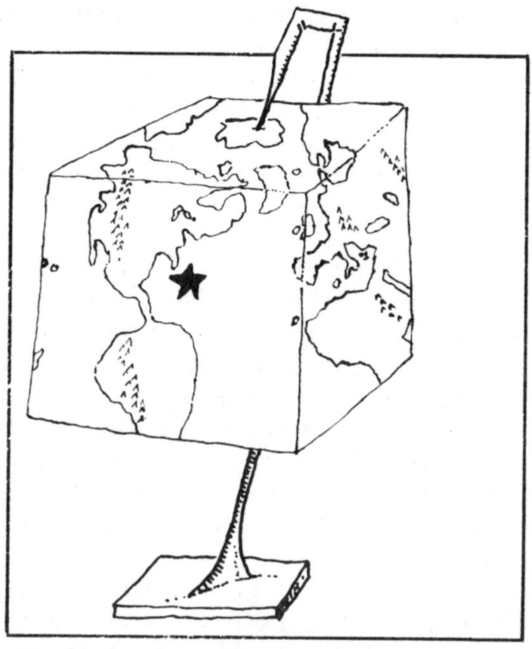

Where's the Cubie's favorite place to buy cigars?
[Cuba]

OMEGA-CUBA
(Importance of the Solution)

As pleasureable as it may be to find a solution, it still isn't the most important aspect of cubing. We feel that too much emphasis has been placed on this single aspect, causing reduced cubing pleasure for millions. This attitude is reflected in locker room talks, like "Wow, did I ever have a great solve the other night" or "I hear there's a cube on the other side of town that gives great solution".

Too much emphasis on solving gives one a very narrow, channeled view of cubing. And automatically excludes giving attention to the many other wonderful elements of intimate cubing. Also, millions of people are simply biologically incapable of solving. Does this mean they can't enjoy cubing? Hardly! Our research shows that some of the most active and happiest cubies are those who can't solve. So don't put too much emphasis on solving, or feel insecure because you can't.

MAGNA CUBUS
(Importance of Cube Size)

As with the ability to solve, the size of the cube is unimportant in determining the possible cubing pleasure. Many people prefer to think that the larger the cube, the greater the pleasure. Again, our research in this area proves that this claim is just a myth. While a larger cube may be easier to manipulate, the pleasure of both the cube and the cubie is no different when a smaller cube is used. Too much emphasis on cube size can detract from the potential cubing experience.

KAMA-TOTU CUBBHA
(Positions)

To spice up your cubing life, try changing positions! It's the easiest, least challenging, least potentially offending way to vary your patterns. You've probably cubed hundreds of times while sitting in an upright position. You've done it so many times you don't even pay attention to your posture and it's effect on your pleasure. Experimenting even a few times with other positions will help make you more aware (and therefore, more receptive to making small changes for the better) of your traditional posture.

Our research shows that many people enjoy cubing while lying on their backs with the cube on top of them. An equal number of people like to lie on top of the cube. Some people like to lie on their stomachs and position the cube on their backs. This makes for difficulties when it comes to solving, but many people still find it extremely rewarding.

If you're the athletic type with strong gymnastic tendencies, you might try cubing while standing or even walking! It's not as impossible as it sounds! We do warn you to exercise caution to avoid running into sharp objects or tripping.

Feel more than free to experiment with a variety of positions. There is no such thing as an immoral position, so give them all a whirl. If a particular position makes you dizzy or hurts your muscles, simply discontinue it. Other positions — once you're in them — will make you laugh so hard you'll forget about cubing. There's certainly nothing wrong with this. In fact, we think a merrily interrupted session of cubing is a healthy thing. It keeps cubing in perspective with other fun pasttimes. One can be too serious about a good thing!

MAYA GORK CUBBHA
(Age of Participants)

One's age has nothing to do with cubing! Anyone can find gratification in cubing — young adults, grandparents, little children, teenagers — why, even young babies enjoy chewing on cubes! The only potential problem might be for senior citizens with dangerous heart conditions. Rumor has it that several people, upon reaching solution, died because of heart attacks. While we do urge people with bad hearts to consult their doctors regarding cubing activities, we can't think of a better way to go, can you?

MAYA-MAYA RIKA-CUBBHA
(Is One Enough? Are Two Too Many?)

Though very few people talk about it openly, our confidential research process has revealed that a large majority of people have a strong desire to partake in cubing with two cubes at one time. These people are not interested in large scale orgies or 'swinging', nor do they wish to foresake the relationship they've developed with their special cube, but they do think the potential benefits of doing two cubes at once (from time to time) are well worth the investigation and experimentation. But for better or worse, very few people ever do try two cubes at one time.

Those who have tried have met with experiences ranging from the terribly bad to the very good. The greatest problem was that it was simply beyond the capacity of most people to successfully manipulate two cubes at one time! Other problems, on behalf of the people, included guilt because of a lack of monogamous faith to their regular cube partner, who, more often than not, was not eager to participate in the adventure but went along nevertheless.

Then there are those who have had very happy experiences with their *menage a trois*! When interviewing these people, we unfortunately got very little information. The person simply sits with a big smile and a faraway look in his eyes.

SODO-YAMAHA CUBBHA
(Sadocubism)

This is a very touchy subject. Please do not interpret our attention to sadocubism as anything more than sharing information about people in all situations. We ourselves do not practice it and have no interest in it. But for those that do wish to practice it, or already do, and even for those who are mildly curious, we will discuss it. We pass no judgement on it's worth, pro, or con. That's for you to decide.

A sadocubist is one who derives pleasure from inflicting pain or humiliation upon the cube. A sadocubist is not necessarily mentally disturbed, though many are. A sadocubist can inflict pain on his cube and yet still have the positive feelings towards that cube that 'wholesome' cubies have towards theirs. It's simply a quirk that some people *happen* to get their kicks in a socially frowned upon manner. And what are the more common manifestations of that manner?

It can begin with light, playful slaps, which quickly become strenuous spankings, and then often lead to whippings of the cube with aids (hitting a cube can be quite painful to the hand). Some cubes are blindfolded and tied to a bedpost or refrigerator handle. Sadocubists have been known to slug, kick, bite and spit on their cubes. Often, the humiliation is given verbally; "You illegitimate son of a sphere!... You're a latent trapezoid, aren't you?..." or, "I should turn you into a two dimensional polygram, and oh, you'd like that, wouldn't you?"

This sort of thing can be quite stimulating to the sadocubist. Though he or she often suffers from severe guilt afterwards, these cubies continue to practice cubing in this manner because it gives such great pleasure. Really, as long as the cube is not bothered, there's no specific danger or harm. There can be problems, our reseach shows, from inability to cope with the guilt. (A cube is very difficult to harm, but don't tell anyone).

If you feel a desire to at least give sadocubism a try, talk openly about it with your cube. Don't be embarrassed or worried. If you have a solid, healthy relationship with your cube, you can talk freely about these things without any fear of recrimination. What's that? You like fear? Read on.

MASOCUBISM

Masocubism, the suffering of pain and humiliation on the part of the cubie as a result of the cube's actions, is a rare practice when compared to sadocubism, mostly because it is very difficult for a cube to do *anything*.

The only form of masocubism we could discover involves having the masocubist tied down by another cubie and having a nearly solved cube placed on his chest or another position where he can't help but see it. No amount of struggling can get that cube solved. It's terrible and cruel and the cubie loves it! After an hour of this the other cubie returns and solves the cube, gives a brief glimpse, then mercilessly scrambles the cube, unties the person and leaves. (If you happen to know of any other practical masocubistic practices, please let us know.)

FANTASIES & CUBIE PORN

Our research has shown that everyone, cubie and cube both, have at least occasional fantasies during the act of cubing. The cubie dreams he's solving three or four cubes at one time, the cube dreams it's giving a young innocent it's first solve. The cubie dreams the cube has sixteen squares to a side, the cube dreams the cubie has no fingers or thumbs. Some fantasies are beautiful, some are ugly. Our opinion, though, is that all fantasies are harmless, and in fact, very often helpful. They should not be repressed or apologized for. In most cases, it is better not to discuss the fantasy with the partner because of — silly as it sounds, considering imaginary source — potential jealousy.

A fantasy is a claim to being a unique entity. This is necessary for the id when one is lost in the communality of passionate cubing. Despite the commonly expressed negative stigma attached to creating fantasies, our research shows you are in fact unhealthy if you don't fantasize!

We suggest that for maximum pleasure, you plan your fantasy before you begin cubing. Imagine your cube is from the rich side of town and has offered you a huge sum of money and is willing to solve itself while.... you get the idea? When it's planned out ahead of time, all you need to do is to enjoy the physical sensations and not spend any time creating on the spur of the moment.

GRAPHUS CUBBHA
(Cubie Porn)

Cubie porn has often been thought of as cheap and ugly, while it is actually an important aid to the mental well being of the person who is presently unattached to a cube. The person can obtain gratification by looking at pictures or videotapes of other cubes being solved, or even cubes solving cubes — anything. Cubie porn provides a necessary placebo in times of need.

For the person who is happily involved with a cube, the benefit of cubie porn is that it provides a more visual grasp for many of that person's fantasies. This is particulary true with the latent sadocubist or masocubist.

Some couples like to cube while viewing cubie porn. More and more couples are using the popular video cassettes of cubie porn movies. They find it a safe, healthy way to live their fantasies. They also enjoy the exhibitionist like element of allowing their partner to see them take pleasure in another couple's cubing.

Is cubie porn for you? All we can suggest is for you to try it and see. If you like it, fine. If you don't, that's fine too. Just be careful not to force your views on your cube, be they pro or con.

ESCAPO CUBBHA
(Alternatives to Cubing)

Like it or not, there are times when you will not be able to cube, either because of medical reasons or any other number of common causes. During these times, it's good to have an alternative pasttime to pursue. We suggest jigsaw puzzles, electronic computer games or tic-tac-toe. They're a lot of fun.

Sadly, some people pursue, as an alternative to cubing, *sex*! We think this is most disgusting. Sex is evil, ugly, nasty and makes people go blind at an early age. It's not even worthy of intelligent discussion. It's the price we pay for our Original Sin. It must only be practiced to conceive children. We are all better off if we lock it in the closet and never talk about it. Ever.

SUMMARY

We hope that our intelligent, mature discussion of a perfectly natural biological function, cubing, will help you derive more pleasure from it's practice. Rational discourse can only be based on full knowledge of facts and reality, and that's all we've tried to present. There's no reason *not* to take the most pleasure possible from cubing. We no longer live in the Dark Ages.